SWINBURNE

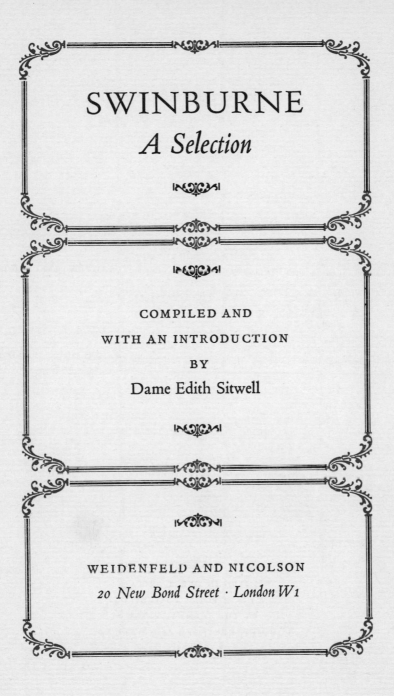

SWINBURNE
A Selection

COMPILED AND

WITH AN INTRODUCTION

BY

Dame Edith Sitwell

WEIDENFELD AND NICOLSON
20 New Bond Street · London W1

PRINTED IN GREAT BRITAIN
IN 13-14 POINT POLIPHILUS
BY THE SHENVAL PRESS
LONDON, HERTFORD AND HARLOW
R 17/6128

This anthology
is dedicated by the compiler to
ALBERTO DE LACERDA
who suggested the making of it
E.S.

Contents

◄◊►

CONTENTS

Introduction

ALGERNON CHARLES SWINBURNE, one of the greatest poets England has produced, was born at 7 Chester Street, Grosvenor Place, at 5.0 am on the 5th April 1837. He was the eldest child of the forty-year-old Charles Henry Swinburne, Captain, and, after his retirement, Admiral in the Royal Navy, and the twenty-seven-year-old Lady Jane Swinburne, née Hamilton, daughter of the 3rd Earl of Ashburnham.

It was a strange family for him to be born into—not because they were aristocrats, a class which has produced, among others, that unsurpassable singing flame Sir Philip Sidney, one of the greatest lyrical poets in our language, and Percy Bysshe Shelley—but because the interests of Swinburne's particular family were entirely absorbed by sport, the navy, and the army.

Father and son were diametrically opposed in character; 'and it is impossible to escape the conclusion', wrote Swinburne's latest biographer Mr Humphrey Hare (*Swinburne, a Biographical Approach,* H. F. and G. Witherby Ltd.), 'that there was a morbid antagonism between father and son'. The latter's childhood cannot, therefore, have been happy, and his early youth even less so, as his father, having been placed on the reserve in 1857, was, from that time onwards, permanently at home.

However, the Admiral tried, as far as his nature permitted, to be just to his son, and even went so far as to make

1

his career as a writer possible, not only by giving him a small allowance, but actually by financing the publication of his early books. He undoubtedly did his duty, and, in later years, when rumours of outstanding riotous behaviour reached him, he would swoop down on his son in rescue‑raids which had a certain war‑like character.

Swinburne's life at Eton can have been no more happy than his home‑life. For there, too, he was surrounded by entirely alien characters. He undoubtedly caused a good deal of amazement, but although other boys would watch him, unable to believe their eyes or ears, 'none dreamt', wrote his cousin Lord Redesdale, 'of interfering with him. He carried with him one magic charm—he was absolutely courageous. He did not know what fear meant.' And Sir George Young, one of his few friends at Eton, said 'There was something a little formidable about him.'

But to counter the story of the non‑bullying of Swinburne at school, I must recall to my readers Sir Osbert Sitwell's report of a conversation an old gentleman of eighty held with him. 'I remember well when I went to Eton,' said the old gentleman, 'the head boy called us together, and, point‑ing to a little fellow with curly red hair, said, "kick him if you are near enough, and if you are not near enough, throw a stone at him". I have often wondered what became of him. His name was Swinburne.'

'In a schoolroom only approached by a sort of ladder,' wrote Sir Edmund Gosse, 'Swinburne's wild and glowing head appeared, one dark morning, very late for school, as if out of the floor. . . . The master in charge . . . paused to exclaim "Ha! Here's the rising sun at last" .'

The amazement he aroused took many forms. On one occasion, when the boys were sentenced to have some medicine inflicted on them in order to ward off colds, a minute creature with scarlet hair was seen dancing madly upon his bed. The matron (or Dame, as these are called at

Eton) feared delirium. But she was reassured. 'It's only little Swinburne, reciting again.'

When he was fifteen years old, 'that lad is a flame of fire!' one of his grandfather's visitors exclaimed, as the boy flashed, hatless, past the windows.

No truer word was ever spoken.

What would, with ordinary men, have been his life (his only real life was in the writing and reading of poetry) seems to have been spent in transports of mental excitement. Even as a boy he would, when reading or reciting poetry, flutter his hands—this being, according to the specialist to whom the alarmed Lady Jane took him, 'the result of an excess of electric vitality'.

With his (according to his cousin, afterwards Lord Redesdale) 'peculiar dancing step, his hair, like the Zazzera of the old Florentines, tossed about by the wind', he raged about the world, screaming with ecstasy, shrieking with fury, espousing causes (the latter had a bad effect on his poetry).

He must, I think, excepting when writing or reading poems, have been acutely unhappy. But perhaps he did not even know this, all his blood and spirit having gone to the making of poetry.

Professor Jacques Maritain, writing of Oscar Wilde in *Art and Poetry*, said, 'To put in his life, not in his work, his genius as an artist, nothing more absurd than this design. . . . It is to carry over into a flute the art of the cithera, into a bird the law of the snow. His life was only a useless phase.'

This was not so with Swinburne. Poetry alone was his existence.

This extraordinary creature, so astonishing in appearance (Henry Adams, in his Autobiography, described him, at the age of twenty-five, as resembling 'in action . . . a tropical bird, high-crested, long-beaked, quick moving, with rapid

3

utterance and screams of humour, quite unlike any English lark or nightingale. One could hardly call him a macaw among owls, and yet no ordinary comparison availed'), had amongst the most wonderful singing-voices and hands for forming poetry of any poet in our language.

I do not propose to enter into the details of this great poet's unhappy life, although there are moments in that life the thought of which I cherish—such as the occasion when, at a house party, Swinburne read aloud 'Les Noyades', a poem not, perhaps, of the highest propriety, and also, it is said, 'The Leper', in the presence of the Archbishop of York—and the short spell of time in which he shared a house with Dante Gabriel Rossetti, William Rossetti and George Meredith.

Mr Humphrey Hare states that Dante Gabriel thought, at one moment, of buying an elephant which could be trained to clean the windows.

I was told by a member of the Prinsep family (whose lives touched, very closely, the lives of the Pre-Raphaelites) that Rossetti did, actually, buy the elephant. One can only begin to speculate on the thoughts that must have passed through that sagacious animal's head when, swab in trunk, he looked through the drawing-room window and wit-nessed (and heard) Swinburne flat on his back on the floor, arms outstretched to heaven, shrieking at the top of his voice, and D. G. Rossetti, in a perpendicular position (hands stretched downwards at his sides in denunciation), emitting loud bass roars.

Life was by no means always peaceful at the house in Chelsea which, forming a band in order to share the expenses, they, and several of the Pre-Raphaelite group, had rented. Meredith was in the habit of preaching sermons to Swinburne on the subject of sobriety, and to Dante Gabriel on the subject of the necessity of taking exercise in order to reduce his figure; and William Morris, who did

4

not live there, but was a constant visitor, was evidently oblivious of William Rossetti's intellectual attainments. In any case, when he brought round 'Sigurd' as a present to Dante Gabriel, the latter said, 'To be honest, Topsy, I can't take much interest in a chap whose father was a dragon!' To which Morris replied, 'I don't see it is any worse than being a man whose brother is a fool!'

Both these anecdotes were told me by Sir Edmund Gosse.

Though Swinburne spent much of his time with the Pre-Raphaelites, he was of a different, and far greater, order of poets. Their minds were, as D. S. MacColl said of Manet in his *Nineteenth Century Painting*, 'that joyful heedless mind of summer, beneath, or above, thought, the intense sensation of life, with its lights and colours, coming and going in the head'.

The Pre-Raphaelites were entirely lacking in passion. Although Swinburne also had 'the intense sensation of life, with its lights and colours, coming and going in the head', he was on fire with passion, was, in himself, as much a fire as was that brand that ended Meleager's life. But the brand that was Swinburne had light, did not crumble into ash.

He was a supreme technician, with an unbelievable mastery over sound, and he was a great tragic poet.

'Is there not', enquired Socrates (Plato: *Cratylus*), 'an essence of colour and of sound as of anything else which may be said to be an essence? . . . And if anyone could imitate the essence of each thing in letters and syllables, would he not express the nature of each thing?'

'It is', wrote Richard Wagner in his book on Beethoven, 'a matter of experience that, by the side of the world that presents itself as visible in waking as well as in dreaming, we are conscious of yet another world which manifests itself by sound . . . a true world of sound by the side of a world of light, of which it may be said that it bears the same relation to the latter as dreaming does to waking.'

It is with this world of sound that these notes, for the most part, will deal.

'It has been experimentally demonstrated', said W. M. N. Sullivan (*The Bases of Modern Science*), 'that light exerts pressure on any body on which it falls. This pressure is due to the momentum of the moving light energy. It has, also, been proved that light has weight.'

Vowels play the part of light or of darkness—consonants that of matter—having 'the most universal qualities of matter . . . such as gravity, cohesion, rigidity, sensitiveness to light'.* Consonants therefore seem, often, to be soaked with light or with darkness.

Again, with regard to the relationship of consonants and vowels, it might, perhaps, be said that the vowels are the spirit, the consonants and labials the physical identity, with all the variations of harshness, hairiness, coldness, rough⁄ ness, smoothness, etc.—(Dante wrote of words being 'shaggy' or 'buttered', 'combed' or 'hairy')—the consonants therefore are 'the garment of the spirit, thus distinguished, marked off and announced . . . to the outer world [as] the animal by the skin, the tree by the bark'. (Wagner: *Opera and Drama*, Vol. II, Prose Works: trans. W. A. Ellis.)

Consonants shape; they do not affect time as do vowels. Although vowels have also their place, position, depth and height, they do not give body.

Francis Bacon, in Century I of his *Natural History*, wrote 'Waters, in the noise they make as they run, represent to the air a trembling noise . . . which trembling as of water hath an affinity with the letter L.'

Swinburne had a great mastery over these liquid sounds, witness the fourth line in the first verse of the Chorus, 'When the hounds of spring are on winter's traces', in

* Schopenhauer: *The World as Will and Idea*.

6

Atalanta in Calydon, where, by the change to the sharp external and internal R's used throughout the verse, from the water-trembling sound of L's in 'lisp of leaves' he seems, actually, to reproduce the sound of rain.

Paul Valéry, in his *Poet's Notebook,* wrote '. . . towards the middle of the nineteenth century, we see asserting itself in our literature a remarkable will to isolate Poetry once for all from every essence but itself. . . . Ordinary spoken language is a practical tool. It is constantly revolving immediate problems. Its task is fulfilled when each sentence has been completely abolished, annulled, and replaced by its meaning. Comprehension is its end. But on the other hand, poetic usage is dominated by *personal* conditions, by a conscious, continuous, and sustained musical feeling.

'Moreover, these conditions usually combine with a careful observance of various technical conventions, whose effect is constantly to remind the versifier that he is not moving within the system of vulgar speech, but in another quite distinct system.

'Here language is no longer a transitive act, an expedient. On the contrary it has its own value, which must remain intact, in spite of the operations of the intellect on its given propositions. Poetic language must preserve itself through itself, and remain the same, not to be altered by the act of intelligence that finds or gives it a meaning.'

In the same work, Valéry wrote 'Thought must be hidden in verse like the nutritive essence in fruit. It is nourishing but seems to be merely delicious. One perceives pleasure only, but one receives a substance. Enchantment, that is the nourishment it contains.'

The ideal of 'isolating poetry once for all from every essence but itself' is found in the Pre-Raphaelites.

But, at the same time, these men, and that far greater poet Swinburne, were born at a time when commonsense reigned, or rather presided over, poetry. There is no such commonsense to be found in Swinburne.

Professor Jacques Maritain, writing of Plato and Poetry*, said 'He never tires of praising mania, or that enthusiasm which abolishes thought. . . . And he expresses a firm and reasoned-out conviction . . . that commonsense is the greatest obstacle to poetry, and that neither concepts nor logic nor rational knowledge have any part in it. And not only the poets, but their listeners also, not only the poem, but also the delight, and the contact with beauty that it brings us, depend on an inspiration superior to reason.'

Plato did not mean, Professor Maritain did not mean, and I, in quoting the latter, do not mean that *thought* is un-necessary to poetry. What is meant is that the everyday commonplace life of the world is not only unnecessary, but fatal to great poetry.

Not only was Swinburne born at a time when common-sense was the most admired of qualities, but also at a time when a hideous insensitivity to sound (coming after the glories of Coleridge, Keats and Shelley)—an insensitivity which, no doubt, was the result in part of the toil-stricken noises, or the wish to escape from these, of industrial England—was the order of the day.

This hideous insensitivity had even, indeed, preceded the toil-stricken era.

At the time when Swinburne's splendours broke upon the world, the public had been completely deafened by such 'horrible and heart-rending cacophonies' (to quote Saints-bury on the subject, not of Burns, the author of the following outrage, but of Mrs Browning) as this:

> O raging fortune's withering blast
> Has laid my leaf full low! O

---

* *Creative Intuition in Art and Poetry*. Harvill Press.

O raging fortune's withering blast
Has laid my leaf full low! O.
My stem was fair, my bud was green,
  My blossom sweet did blow; O
The dew fell fresh, the sun rose mild,
  And made my branches grow; O.
But luckless fortune's northern storms
  Laid a' my blossoms low, O
But luckless fortune's northern storms
  Laid a' my blossoms low, O!

Let us compare this hideous rumpus with the second line
of this stanza from 'Laus Veneris':

Ah yet would God this flesh of mine might be
Where air might wash and long leaves cover me,
  Where tides of grass break into foam of flowers,
Or where the wind's feet shine along the sea.

This, with its stretching sound of 'where air' and the sound
of 'long leaves', prolonging the line, could only have been
produced by a great technician. (The assonances of 'where
air' are of a faintly different length.)

So deafened were the public by Burns' singularly unfortunate verse, and by other horrors, that they were unhearing
of Swinburne's transcendental music. They were willing to
take shelter from the blasts of the meaningless, breath-
destroying O's used by Burns in the above verse, with the
shrunken, teetering, wriggling, oily productions, or powder-
dry concoctions, the synthetic tears (every tear concealing a
snigger), of Austin Dobson, who was Swinburne's junior
by three years, and who was guilty of such lines as these,
culled from an embarrassing work called 'Good-night,
Babette'.

B   9

M. Vieuxbois

Where *have you* been?

Babette

Why, M'sieu knows:—

April!... Ville d'Avray... Ma'amselle Rose!

M. Vieuxbois

Ah, I am old and I forget,

Was the place growing green, Babette?

Babette

But of a greenness!—Yes, M'sieu!

And then the sky so blue—so blue!

And when I dropped my *immortelle*

How the birds sang!

(Lifting her apron to her eyes)

This poor Ma'amselle.

The rest of this baby-talk is just as nauseating.

It is not surprising, therefore, that people stuffed with this cheap confectionery were unaware of the fire-music, the bird-music of Swinburne, or those lines which, as he said of Rossetti (but the phrase is far more applicable to his own poetry), are 'sinuous as water or as light, flexible and penetrative, delicate and rapid'.

The same hideous insensitiveness to sound prevails at this time. Somebody, writing of Thomas Nashe recently, referred to '... the celebrated verses with the line now amended to:

"Brightness falls from the *hair*" '

[Italics mine].

Really! Amended by *whom*, may I ask? Nashe was, after all, a poet. Is it likely that he would have bothered to write down that dreary platitude?

Also we should remember this phrase from Longinus' 'On the Sublime', 'Beautiful words are the very and peculiar light of the mind'.

The unfortunate general public must be greatly bewildered!

A gentleman named Robin Skelton, for instance, writing admiringly of certain new proletarian versifiers, declared 'The language they use is hard and strong as the pavements on which they walk, and as vigorous and direct as the people they live with.'

He then quotes

> Molly Vickers
> Wets her knickers
> Georgie's father's big and black.
> Cream on Sunday,
> Milk on Monday,
> I'm the cock of all the back.

While the public is taught to take this seriously, or such lines as these:

> Is it, when paper roses make us sneeze,
> A mental or a physical event?

and while they are assured seriously by a critic, Mr F. W. Bateson, in a book called *English Poetry*, that poetry is, 'in its essence, simply a part, in some respects a culmination, of the process of social living, one of those things like law-abidingness, and politeness, voting at a General Election, or reading the newspaper'—there is not much hope that poetry as an art, the sound of poetry as an art, will reach them, much less be understood.

In *Under the Microscope*, Swinburne spoke of 'the confidence with which men who have no sense whatever of verbal music, will pronounce judgment on the subtlest question relating to that form of art. A man whose ear is conscious of no difference between Offenbach and Beethoven does not usually stand up as a judge of instrumental music: but there is no ear so hirsute . . . so pointed or so long, that its hearer will not feel himself qualified to pass sentence on the musical rank of any poet's verse, the relative range of his metrical power or skill.'

Swinburne's great metrical powers were, during his lifetime, and are at this time, subjected to much abuse.

Mr Ezra Pound, who has written more finely than any other poet, any other critic, of Swinburne, said 'No one else has made such music in English, I mean has made his kind of music, and it is a music which will compare with Chaucer's "Hide Absolam thy gilte tresses clere" or with any other maker you like.'

There are two kinds of great poetry. There is that which M. Marcel Raymond, in *De Baudelaire au Surréalisme* (one of the most important books of criticism written in our time), called '*l'alchimie poétique . . . ces rencontres fulgurantes de vocables qu'ébranlent l'être d'un coup comme l'électricité du Réel*'.

Swinburne was a poet of '*l'alchimie poétique*'.

The other kind of great poet is that of which Valéry wrote, in *L'Introduction à la Méthode*: '*Dans tous les vers réside une profonde note de l'existence qui donne, dès qu'on l'écoute, toutes les complications des conditions et des variétés de l'existence.*'

The '*existence quotidienne*' with its complications and varieties we shall not find in Swinburne.

The light by which he worked was an unappeasable fire.

I think he suffered greatly: 'I live on my death,' said Michelangelo (quoted by Adrian Stokes), 'and he who does not know how to live on anxiety and death, let him come into the fire in which I am consumed.'

His was the alchemy of the word.

Paul Valéry said, of Victor Hugo, 'Often with him the development of a poem is visibly deduced from a wonderful accident of language that has occurred in his mind'.

Mr John Press, in his remarkable book *The Fire and the Fountain*, after speaking of the experiences of Tennyson and Yeats, wrote 'We begin to understand that the genesis of a poem may be a single word, a group of words, or even a particular rhythm in which no individual words are clearly distinguishable. Such an idea is, indeed, quite incomprehensible if we think that a poem is the translation of a thought or of an emotion into words, but there is a great deal of evidence which suggests that this process of translation does not always take place, and that a poem may unfold like a flower from the bud of a single word.'

With Swinburne the generation was usually from a rhythm.

'Let the candidate [he who would become a poet]', wrote Mr Pound, 'fill his mind with the finest cadences he can discover, preferably in a foreign language, so that the meaning of the words may be less likely to divert his attention from the movement.'

This statement will, of course, evoke a loud howl from persons who know nothing of poetry, or of the means by which poetry is generated.

Mr Pound did not mean, and I, in quoting him, do not mean, that poetry should be devoid of sense. But just as it is of no use for a person, no matter how beautiful his soul may be, to play the piano if he has no gift for playing the piano, and has never troubled to learn how to do so, it is useless for persons to try to write poetry unless they have practised it technically.

To pretend that Swinburne's poems are devoid of thought

is unspeakably ridiculous—witness the transcendentally
great choruses of 'Atalanta in Calydon' and these verses
from 'Félise', a poem not given in the body of the book
because it was not, throughout, amongst his most perfect,
but which contains great beauties.

. . . .

Kiss me once hard as though a flame
  Lay on my lips and made them fire;
The same lips now, and not the same;
  What breath shall fill and re-inspire
  A dead desire?

The old song sounds hollower in mine ear
  Than thin keen sounds of dead men's speech—
A noise one hears and would not hear;
  Too strong to die, too weak to reach
  From wave to beach.

We stand on either side the sea,
  Stretch hands, blow kisses, laugh and lean
I toward you, you toward me;
  But what hears either save the keen
  Grey sea between?

A year divides us, love from love,
  Though you love now, though I loved then.
The gulf is strait, but deep enough;
  Who shall recross, who among men
  Shall cross again?

. . . .

So this thing is, and must be so;
  For man dies, and love also dies.

14

Though yet love's ghost moves to and fro
  The sea-green mirrors of your eyes,
  And laughs, and lies.

Eyes coloured like a water-flower,
  And deeper than the green sea's glass;
Eyes that remember one sweet hour—
  In vain we swore it should not pass;
  In vain, alas!

Ah my Félise, if love or sin,
  If shame or fear could hold it fast,
Should we not hold it? Love wears thin,
  And they laugh well who laugh the last.
  Is it not past?

The gods, the gods are stronger; time
  Falls down before them, all men's knees
Bow, all men's prayers and sorrows climb
  Like incense towards them; yea, for these
  Are gods, Félise.

Immortal are they, clothed with powers,
  Not to be comforted at all;
Lords over all the fruitless hours;
  Too great to appease, too high to appal,
  Too far to call.

For none shall move the most high gods,
  Who are most sad, being cruel; none
Shall break or take away the rods
  Wherewith they scourge us, not as one
  That smites a son.

By many a name of many a creed
　We have called upon them, since the sands
Fell through time's hour-glass first, a seed
　Of life; and out of many lands
　Have we stretched hands.

When have they heard us? who hath known
　Their faces, climbed unto their feet,
Felt them and found them? Laugh or groan,
　Doth heaven remurmur and repeat
　Sad sounds or sweet?

Do the stars answer? in the night
　Have ye found comfort? or by day
Have ye seen gods? What hope, what light,
　Falls from the farthest starriest way
　On you that pray?

Are the skies wet because we weep
　Or fair because of any mirth?
Cry out; they are gods; perchance they sleep;
　Cry; thou shalt know what prayers are worth,
　Thou dust and earth.

O earth, thou art fair; O dust, thou art great;
　O laughing lips and lips that mourn,
Pray, till ye feel the exceeding weight
　Of God's intolerable scorn,
　Not to be borne.

·　·　·　·　·　·　·

'It is sometimes said', Swinburne wrote in his essay on

Dante Gabriel Rossetti, 'that a man may have a strong and perfect style who has nothing to convey worth conveyance under cover of it. This is indeed a favourite saying of men who have no words in which to convey the thoughts which they have not, of men born dumb who express by grunts and clichés the inexpressible eloquence which is not in them, and would fain seem to labour in miscarriage of ideas which they have never conceived. But it remains for them to prove as well as assert that beauty and power of expression can accord with emptiness or sterility of matter, or that impotence of articulation must imply depth and wealth of thought.'

At his best, at his greatest, Swinburne was a poet who produced the pure essence of poetry.

Professor Maritain, in *Creative Intuition in Art and Poetry*, wrote*:

'... it might be said, it seems to me, that that element in beauty which is *integrity* has principally to do with poetic intuition as objectivizing itself into the action or the theme, whereas that element which is *radiance* has principally to do with its native and original state. Hence it is that poetic intuition may happen to appear with striking radiance even in a poem lacking in integrity, and such splintered fragments, transparent to the rays of being, may be enough to reveal the pure essence of poetry. For nothing is more precious than a capture on the high seas of poetry, be it offered in a single line:

> *L'espoir luit comme un brin de paille dans l'étable.*
> (Verlaine in 'L'espoire luit'. *Sagesse*)

> O thou steeled cognizance whose leap commits
> The agile precincts of the lark's return.
> (Crane in Atalanta: *The Bridge*)

* Pages 134 and 135.

Odour of blood when Christ was slain
Made all Platonic tolerance vain.
(Yeats in *Two Songs from a Play*.)

Professor Maritain continues: 'And I shall always prefer
a haikai [? E.S.] if it has this kind of transparency, to a
big noisy machine deafening me with ideas.'

Swinburne's exquisite songs are of this transparency.
Single lines float towards us and remain in our memory.
(Of these songs I shall write later.) But his greatest poem,
'Atalanta in Calydon', has complete unity. The beings in
it are phantoms from Thebes or Cyclopean cities, yet have
tides of blood beating in their veins. But with this unity, the
tremendous choruses—mankind voicing its despair, defying
an unhearing heaven—have, as Nietzsche said of the birth
of tragedy, 'The rapture of the Dionysian state, the annihila-
tion of the ordinary bounds and limits of existence'.

The sounds, in Swinburne's most wonderful works—to
quote from Francis Bacon's *Naturall History*—seem to be
'Emissions of Beames from the Object seen; almost like
Odours, save that they are more incorporeall'.

There are but few influences of the poetry of the past to be
found in Swinburne. An echo of Marlowe in 'St Dorothy',
and, in such poems as 'A Ballad of Life', in which he wore
his 'golden singing-coat', there is a certain inheritance from
that great poet Gavin Douglas—witness these lines from
Douglas's *King Hart I (XLVIII—LIII)*:

The courtines all of gold about the bed
Weill stentit* was, quhair fair Dame Plesaunce lay;
Than new Desyr, als gredie as ane glede†
Come rinnand in, and made ane grit deray.

* Stentit, drawn.   † Glede, kite.

18

'Yeild you, madame' grene Lust culd say all sone:
'And fairlie sall we governe you and youris,
Our Lord King Hartis will most now be done,
Thay yet is law among the bouris.'*

The relationship is distant, but I think it exists.

But, for the most part, he is a tragic poet. 'Walking', as Blake said of himself (in 'Marriage of Heaven and Hell'), 'among the fires of Hell, delighted with the enjoyments of genius, which to Angels look like torments and insanity', he had, technically, at his greatest—to quote once more from Blake, but from a different work—'Satan's mathe׳ matic Holiness, Length, Bredth and Heighth'.

It was, perhaps, the flawless majesty of the poem 'Faus׳ tine'—in which the only variation is produced by the change from the bright sounds of the second syllable of 'Faustine' and its absolute rhymes, and the recurring dimming disson׳ ances of 'kiss', 'sin', 'win', 'therein', etc.—that caused, according to Saintsbury, a certain German critic to accuse Swinburne of monotony. The answer to that charge is the infinite variation to be found in 'Atalanta in Calydon', where, at times, the speeches flicker to and fro like flames.

The lack of variation in the line׳endings of 'Faustine' give it, in part, its majesty.

Swinburne, often as great a critic as he was a poet, wrote in *Essays and Studies*, 'Variety is a rare and high quality; but poets of the first order have had little or none of it, witness Keats and Coleridge'. [Shakespeare, perhaps, was the great exception—E.S.]

But Swinburne had great metrical variety. He had, at moments, what Sir Kenneth Clark, writing of Leonardo da Vinci's 'Leda' in his book on *The Nude*, called 'a tropical redundancy of rhythm'. This—and it is very lovely

* Bouris, chambers.

—is to be found in such poems as 'The Two Dreams'. At other moments his rhythms were as hard, the texture as dark, as porphyry. An example of the latter is 'Faustine', which is a miracle of technique throughout, and a great tragic poem.

The stanzas I am about to quote are, I think, as great as anything to be found in 'Laus Veneris'. The poem belongs to the mineral kingdom, '*J'existe toujours comme le basalte.... C'est un homme ou une pierre qui commence le ... chant?*' (*Chants de Maldoror.*)

Stanzas from 'Faustine'
Ave Faustina Imperatrix, morituri te salutant.

Lean back, and get some minutes' peace;
  Let your head lean
Back to the shoulder with its fleece
  Of locks, Faustine.

The shapely silver shoulder stoops,
  Weighed over clean
With state of splendid hair that droops
  Each side, Faustine.

Let me go over your good gifts
  That crown you queen;
A queen whose kingdom ebbs and shifts
  Each week, Faustine.

Bright heavy brows well gathered up:
  White gloss and sheen;
Carved lips that make my lips a cup
  To drink, Faustine.

Wine and rank poison, milk and blood,
  Being mixed therein
Since first the devil threw dice with God
  For you, Faustine.

Your naked new-born soul, their stake,
  Stood blind between;
God said 'let him that wins her take
  And keep Faustine'.

But this time Satan throve, no doubt;
  Long since, I ween,
God's part in you was battered out;
  Long since, Faustine.

The die rang sideways as it fell,
  Rang cracked and thin,
Like a man's laughter heard in hell
  Far down, Faustine.

A shadow of laughter like a sigh,
  Dead sorrow's kin;
So rang, thrown down, the devil's die
  That won Faustine.

A suckling of his breed you were,
  One hard to wean;
But God, who lost you, left you fair,
  We see, Faustine.

You have the face that suits a woman
  For her soul's screen—
The sort of beauty that's called human
  In hell, Faustine.

You could do all things but be good
   Or chaste of mien;
And that you would not if you could,
   We know, Faustine.

Even he who cast seven devils out
   Of Magdalene
Could hardly do as much, I doubt,
   For you, Faustine.

Did Satan make you to spite God?
   Or did God mean
To scourge with scorpions for a rod
   Our sins, Faustine?

.   .   .   .

Your drenched loose hands were stretched to hold
   The vine's wet green,
Long ere they coined in Roman gold
   Your face, Faustine.

.   .   .   .

Stray breaths of Sapphic song that blew
   Through Mitylene
Shook the fierce quivering blood in you
   By night, Faustine.

The shameless nameless love that makes
   Hell's iron gin
Shut on you like a trap that breaks
   The soul, Faustine.

And when your veins were void and dead,
    What ghosts unclean
Swarmed round the straitened barren bed
    That hid Faustine?

What sterile growths of sexless root
    Or epicine?
What flower of kisses without fruit
    Of love, Faustine?

What adders came to shed their coats?
    What coiled obscene
Small serpents with soft stretching throats
    Caressed Faustine?

But the time came of famished hours,
    Maimed loves and mean,
This ghastly thin-faced time of ours,
    To spoil Faustine.

You seem a thing that hinges hold,
    A love-machine
With clockwork joints of supple gold—
    No more, Faustine.

Not godless, for you serve one God,
    The Lampsacene,
Who metes the gardens with his rod;
    Your lord, Faustine.

.   .   .   .

That clear hair heavily bound back,
The lights wherein
Shift from dead blue to burnt⁄up black;
Your throat, Faustine,

Strong, heavy, throwing out the face
And hard bright chin
And shameful scornful lips that grace
Their shame, Faustine.

Curled lips, long since half kissed away,
Still sweet and keen;
You'd give him—poison shall we say?
Or what, Faustine?

In the body of the book I have included the two superb
translations from Villon, rather than the whole of Faustine,
since they are less well known.

'Whatever has black sounds, has "duende" '—Manuel
Torres, 'a man of exemplary blood⁄culture', uttered 'this
splendid phrase' to Frederico Garcia Lorca.* Garcia adds
'These black sounds are the mystery, the roots that probe
through the mire that we all know of, and do not under⁄
stand, but which furnish us with whatever is sustaining in
art.'

The mire, perhaps, is only another word for the blood
and this duende sounds in Faustine.

Sometimes, although rarely, his transcendental technique
would, in his less great poems, run away with him. And
then his rhythms gallop, or he uses rocking⁄horse
rhythms, yet at the same time, he is bound by iron fetters.
He cannot descend from the horse until the horse is tired;
nor can he leave the rocking⁄horse until the latter comes to
a stop of its own volition. (Werner Jaeger, in 'Paidezza',

* Appendices to *A Poet in New York*, translated by Ben Belet. Thames
and Hudson.

translated by Gilbert Hignet, speaks of Prometheus in Aeschylus' tragedy, who is chained immovably in iron fetters, and who says 'I am bound here in this rhythm'.) 'Dolores', in my opinion a bad poem, had a rocking-horse for Pegasus.

Professor Maritain said, in *Art and Poetry*,* 'Beauty has not come to the end of its submission to the shameful ascendancy of the God Aesthetics taken as the ultimate end of human life. The interminable, incoercible, appalling laugh of Oscar Wilde consigning a man to sin [Professor Maritain's note c.f. André Gide *Si le grain ne meurt*] still passes like a voluble cry over our arts. It is this that freezes them in their frenzy.'

And 'Dolores' *is* frozen.

Isidore Ducasse, in his Preface to his Poems, wrote '*Oui, je veux proclaimer le beau sur une lyre d'or, défalcation faite des tristesses goitreuse et des fiertés stupides qui décomposent, à sa source, la poésie marécageuse de ce siècle*'.

Swinburne's detractors cannot be blamed for disliking this poem. It is not, however, '*de la poésie marécageuse*', but hard as hell.

He was a supreme master of rhyme.

Walt Whitman, in his Preface to *Leaves of Grass,* wrote 'the profit of rhyme is that it drops seeds of sweeter and more luxuriant rhyme; and of uniformity that it conveys itself into its own roots in the ground out of sight. The rhyme and uniformity of perfect poems show the free growth of metrical laws, and bud from them as unerringly and loosely as lilacs or roses on a bush, and take shapes as compact as the shapes of chestnuts and oranges and melons and pears, and shed the perfume impalpable to form'.

So it is with Swinburne's finest rhymed poems.

In his great poems, the rhythms are never superimposed.

† *Editions Poetry*, London. Nicholson and Watson.

Superimposed rhythms and superimposed rhymes had an unfortunate effect on him, as in these lines from 'Satia Te Sanguine':

> If you loved me ever so little,
>   I could bear the bonds that gall,
> I could dream the bonds were brittle;
>   You do not love me at all.

This is deeply unfortunate; and I cannot imagine how so great a master of verbal music could have brought himself to write it.

Superimposed rhymes—sounds not arising from the necessities of the subject—produced such inferior verses as this, from 'Before the Mirror' (written under a picture and inscribed to Whistler):

> White rose in red rose-garden
>   Is not so white;
> Snow-drops that plead for pardon
>   And pine for fright
> Because the hard East blows
> Over their maiden rows
>   Grow not as this face grows
>   from pale to bright.

'Snowdrops that plead for pardon' was put there because of the rhyme, and is just silly. Pardon from whom? Pardon for what?

Nor, I think, did this poem convey the atmosphere of the picture. There is not the usual 'Emission of Beames' characteristic of all his greater poems, whether long or short.

This poem is too corporeal.

Arthur Symons, a great, but now almost forgotten critic, said that Whistler gave 'aspects of people and things on which a butterfly seems to have left a little of its coloured dust as it alights and pauses. . . . They have their brief

coloured life like butterflies, and with the same momentary perfection. . . .' (*Studies in Seven Arts*). And he spoke
of 'A white which is the soul of a colour, caught and fixed
there by some incalculable but precisely coloured magic.
It ends, of course, by being the ghost of a colour . . . but all
things end, when their particular life is over, by becoming
the ghost of a colour.'

In this particular poem, there is no ghost of a colour.

Swinburne's use of female endings was frequently
wonderful. But what are we to think of the following verse
from 'The Triumph of Time'?

> I shall never be friends again with roses;
>   I shall loathe sweet tunes, where a note grown strong
> Relents and recoils, and climbs and closes,
>   As a wave of the sea turned back by song.
> There are sounds where the soul's delight takes fire,
> Face to face with its own desire;
> A delight that rebels, a desire that reposes;
>   I shall hate sweet music my whole life long.

This poem has been much admired, and has been included
in many anthologies. I think it gives no indication of the
greatness of this poet. It contains, however, the following
stanza, which has a certain beauty:

> There lived a singer in France of old
>   By the tideless dolorous midland sea.
> In a land of sand and ruin and gold
>   There shone one woman, and none but she.
> And finding life for her love's sake fail,
> Being fain to see her, he bade set sail,
> Touched land, and saw her as life grew cold,
>   And praised God, seeing; and so died he.

As regards *line-endings,* the use of the word 'roses' in the plural had an unfortunate effect on his poetry, prosodically, as in the first four lines of 'A Ballad of Dreamland':

> I hid my heart in a nest of roses,
> Out of the sun's way, hidden apart;
> In a softer bed than the soft white snow's is,
> Under the roses I hid my heart.

Here, not only is the poet upon his rocking-horse, but the sounds of 'roses' 'snow's is' 'roses', put so closely together, give the verse a huddled, cramped feeling.

But after the first four lines, the poem recovers itself, and is very beautiful.

> Why would it sleep not? why should it start,
> When never a leaf of the rose-tree stirred?
> What made sleep flutter his wings and part?
> Only the song of a secret bird.

> Lie still, I said, for the wind's wing closes,
> And mild leaves muffle the keen sun's dart;
> Lie still, for the wind on the warm sea dozes,
> And the wind is unquieter yet than thou art.
> Does a thought in thee still as a thorn's wound smart?
> Does the fang still fret thee of hope deferred?
> What bids the lids of thy sleep dispart?
> Only the song of a secret bird.

> The green land's name that a charm encloses,
> It never was writ in the traveller's chart,
> And sweet on its trees as the fruit that grows is,
> It never was sold in the merchant's mart.
> The swallows of dreams through its dim fields dart,
> And sleep's are the tunes in its tree-tops heard;
> No hound's note wakens the wildwood hart,
> Only the song of a secret bird.

Envoi

In the world of dreams I have chosen my part.
  To sleep for a season and hear no word
Of true love's truth or of light love's art,
  Only the song of a secret bird.

(The origin, the germ of the poem was, Swinburne said, the line 'Only the song of a secret bird', by which he was haunted.)

One reason for the failure of the first four lines is, I think, the slipping, sliding 's' sounds—'snow's is' used as a line⁄ending.

The varied uses Swinburne has made of alliteration and assonances, is largely responsible for the beauty of the rest of the poem.

When, as in the last stanza of 'A Ballad of Life', Swin⁄burne does not use the word 'roses' as a line⁄end, he pro⁄duces marvels:

Forth, balad, and take roses in both arms,
  Even till the top rose touch thee in the throat
Where the least thornprick harms;
  And girdled in thy golden singing⁄coat,
Come thou before my lady and say this;
  Borgia, thy gold hair's colour burns in me,
  Thy mouth makes beat my blood in feverish
                                rhymes;
  Therefore so many as these roses be,
  Kiss me so many times.
Then it may be, seeing how sweet she is,
  That she will stoop herself none otherwise
    Than a blown vine⁄branch doth,
  And kiss thee with soft laughter on thine eyes,
    Ballad, and on thy mouth.

As Mr Pound wrote, 'The splendid lines mount up in

one's memory, and overwhelm any minute restrictions of one's praise'.

In 'Rosamond', the first drama Swinburne finished after his boyhood (it was begun in 1857, then torn up, revised, put aside again, and not completed until 1860), there are lines foreshadowing, though how faintly! the last transcen-dental stanza of 'A Ballad of Life':

> God help! Your hair burns to me like gold
> Burnt to pure heat, your colour seen turns in me
> To pain and plague upon the temple vein
> That aches as if the sun's heat snapt the blood
> In hot mid-measure.

To return to Swinburne's rose-theme (not used as a line-end), in the following lines from 'The Two Dreams', the word 'roses' produces a certain softness in the midst of the long and poignant assonances 'grate', 'daily', 'rain', 'deep', 'weeks', 'green', 'leaves', used with an uttermost perfection:

> She, where a gold grate shut the roses in,
> Dwelt daily through deep summer weeks, through
> > green
> Flushed hours of rain upon the leaves;

Another use of the rose-theme occurs in this transcendental passage from 'Anactoria' (one of the greatest of his poems, however much, if we except the memory of the poet who was its theme, we may regret certain lines in the body of the poem):

> Thee too the years shall cover; thou shalt be
> As the rose born of one same blood with thee,
> As a song sung, as a word said, and fall
> Flower-wise, and be not any more at all,
> Nor any memory of thee anywhere;
> For never Muse has bound above thine hair

The high Pierian flower whose graft outgrows
The summer kinship of the mortal rose.

Dryden, in his Dedication to the Æneid, said 'Dampier has informed us, in his *Voyages*, that the air of the country which produces gold is never wholesome.'

I have a strong dislike of the unwholesome air of 'Hermaphroditus' (the air of a country which never produced gold).

The air surrounding the poem 'Anactoria'—a land in which we may find much gold—is, at times, extremely unwholesome. I have omitted such parts of it (both from the body of the book and this Preface) of which this can be said, since—leaving all else aside—they add nothing to the beauty of the poem. But such lines as I have given are wonderful, flawless poetry, as when Sappho, speaking of Venus, says

Nay, sweet, for is she God alone? hath she
Made earth and all the centuries of the sea,
Taught the sun ways to travel, woven most fine
The moonbeams, shed the starbeams forth as wine,
Bound with her myrtles, beaten with her rods,
The young men and the maidens and the gods?
Have we not lips to love with, eyes for tears,
And summer and flower of women and of years?
Stars for the food of morning, and for noon
Sunlight, and exaltation of the moon;
Waters that answer waters, fields that wear
Lilies, and languor of the Lesbian air?

To take the darker portions of the poem:

For who shall change with prayers or thanksgivings
The mystery of the cruelty of things?
Or say what God above all gods and years,
With offering and blood-sacrifice of tears,

With lamentation from strange lands, from graves
Where the snake pastures, from scarred mouths of
slaves,
From prison, and from plunging prows of ships
Through flamelike foam of the sea's closing lips—
With thwartings of strange signs, and wind-blown
hair
Of comets, desolating the dim air,
When darkness is made fast with seals and bars,
And fierce reluctance of disastrous stars,
Eclipse, and sound of shaken hills, and wings
Darkening, and blind inexpiable things—
With sorrow of labouring moons, and altering light
And travail of the planets of the night,
And weeping of the weary Pleiads seven,
Feeds the mute melancholy lust of heaven?

Here, the beauties come, very largely, from alliteration, from
Swinburne's vowel-technique, including the use of the same
vowel, alternately dulled, then sharp, then dark, as in the
lines:
With lamentation from strange lands, from graves
Where the snake pastures, from scarred mouths of slaves.
an effect which gives a strange, waving, wandering movement, slowed, too, because of the many 'S's.
This is followed by the strongly marked alliteration of:
'From prison, and from plunging prows of ships'.
Swinburne, in this poem, varies the actual movement of the
line, time and again, by means of his power over alliteration,
by his perpetual shifting of the alliteration from one part of
a line to another. For instance, the movement of the line
'Where the snake pastures, from scarred mouths of slaves'
is different from that of the next line,
'From prison, and from plunging prows of ships'
and this change is due, not only to the change of accent, but

also to the fact that the alliterations are put in different parts
of the line.

It is also, in this case, a fact that Swinburne foretells, in
the first line, the alliteration of the second line. The movement of the second line quoted differs slightly, though only
slightly, from that of
'And weeping of the weary Pleiads seven',
because, although 'weeping' and 'weary' are put in the same
places in the line as 'prison' and 'plunging', there is no third
alliteration in that line.

Again, the movement of
'And weeping of the weary Pleiads seven,'
with its melting sound, is not the same as that of the thicker
'Feeds the mute melancholy lust of heaven',
where, again, the alliteration is shifted.

Both these lines have a different movement from that of
the last line of the following fragment:

Of me the high God hath not all his will.
Blossom of branches, and on each high hill
Clear air and wind, and under in clamorous vales
Fierce noises of the fiery nightingales,
Buds burning in the sudden spring like fire,
The wan washed sand and the waves' vain desire.

Here, in this last line, the alliteration of external and internal
letters (the varying 'wa's' and 'an's') makes the line more
heavy and weary than if the alliteration were external only;
whilst, at the same time, the change from dulled to bright
'a's' gives a wandering effect. 'Washed', by the way, is
slightly darker than 'wan' because of the 'sh'.

But there is no miracle that is not performed by this great
poet in the excerpts given from 'Anactoria' in this present
book.

Sometimes he makes a change between the movement of
one line and another by the use of the same letter placed,

first externally, then internally and very close together, as in
the third line of this fragment:

> Him would I reach, him smite, him desecrate,
> Pierce the cold lips of God with human breath,
> And mix his immortality with death.

His virtuosity in the varied use of the caesura, his knowledge
of the means by which this will change the movement of a
line, can be compared with the virtuosity of Dryden and of
Pope. With all three poets, the pauses seem of natural
growth—they have varying heights, depths, and lengths.
The difference made by these natural pauses and changes of
accent are of a very subtle kind. Take these beautiful lines:

> Why hath he made us? What had all we done
> That we should live and loathe the sterile sun,
> And with the moon wax paler as she wanes,
> And pulse by pulse feel time grow through
>   our veins?
> Thee too the years shall cover; thou shalt be
> As the rose born of one same blood with thee,

'Laus Veneris' is, to my mind less beautiful than the parts
of 'Anactoria' which I have quoted; but it attains an equal
perfection.

No possible variation made by the use of a pause, a
caesura, no possible lengthening of a line by the use of
certain consonants, liquids, and vowels, is excluded from
this poem, and Swinburne gives a feeling of flawless poise
by his use of alliteration, by his use of assonance and disson-
ance, coming from time to time:

> Lo, this is she that was the world's delight;

> The old grey years were parcels of her might;

34

2

The strewings of the ways wherein she trod

2

Were the twain seasons of the day and night.

Then there is the subtlety with which he changes the heat
and burden, caused by the heavy vowels, into softness, by
the use of un-sharp 'e's' and 'i's,' as in the last line of this
quatrain:

Outside it must be winter among men;
For at the gold bars of the gates again
I heard all night and all the hours of it
The wind's wet wings and fingers drip with rain.

Here again the last line is a miracle of the use of alliteration
and assonances.

Reading such poems as 'Anactoria', 'A Ballad of Life'
and 'The Leper', I am reminded of certain passages in the
singularly beautiful Second and Fourth Books of Paracelsus
—although for the Leper of Swinburne's poem, who, for
the sake of love, existed in 'a poor wattled house', living on
well-water and the seeds of grasses, there could be no
quintessence of gold.

'In the matter of medicine', wrote Paracelsus, 'we have
seen a man sustain himself many years by the quintessence
of gold, taking each day scarcely half a scruple of it.'

Also of these passages from the Fourth Book:

'. . . furthermore, we bear witness that the quintessence
of gold exists in very small quantity, and what remains is a
leprous body wherein is no sweetness or sourness, and no
virtue or piece remains save a mixture of the four elements . . .

'One essence is more powerful for curing leprosy. The
quintessence of juniper expels it. And the quintessence of
amber, the quintessence of antimony, and the quintessence
of gold . . . But the quintessence of the Sun . . . takes away
from the roots all the symptoms of leprosy and renovates the

body as honey and wax are purged and purified by the honeycomb.'

These passages, and another from Paracelsus, inspired a modern poet to write:

> . . . once hold
> The primal matter of all gold—
> From which it grows
> (That Rose of the world) as the sharp clear
>   tree from the seed of the great rose—
>
> Then give of this, condensed to the transparency
> Of the beryl, the weight of twenty barley grains:
> And the leper's face will be full of the rose's face
> After great rains.

'Atalanta in Calydon' is, I think, indisputably Swinburne's greatest work. Here there are no redundancies—there is none of the fatal fluency which marred some of his poems. The work has a grandeur not excelled by any poet since the dramatists of the Elizabethan and Jacobean eras. As Saints bury said, in the third volume of his *History of English Prosody*, 'Every weapon and every sleight of the English poet—equivalence and substitution, alternation and repetition, rhymes and rhymeless suspension of sound, volley and check of verse, stanza construction, line and pause mould ing, foot conjunction and contrast—this poet knows and can use them all. . . . He seems to revel in variety: the stanzas actually hide, though they never falsify, their heredity of norm. But is this variety merely a clever disguise of in ability to preserve and support a severer form? Not in the least. The great—it is not rash to call it the immortal— "Before the beginning of years" comes at once to show the poet.'

To consider certain of the shorter poems.

The strange softness and languor, together with the extreme poignancy of 'Ilicet', are nothing short of miracu lous. Swinburne obtains this effect, to some degree, by the fact that in these stanzas six lines, lines A and B, D and E, have female endings (used very differently from those in the verse I have quoted from the first four lines of 'A Ballad of Dreamland', and the verse quoted from 'The Triumph of Time'). The female endings of 'Ilicet' are usually devoid of poignant vowels (and when the vowel *is* poignant, it is invariably, with one exception, a high A, thus giving the effect of something trying to raise itself from the dust). Lines C and F have common endings with, nearly always, poignant vowels.

In the final stanza, however, the last syllable of the female endings do not drop until after a long and fierce cry: 'retire', 'desire', and here these syllables are less dropping than stretching outward; so that it seems as if the dust is gathering together in one last effort to raise itself from the tomb. The common endings in this verse are very dark and deep: 'call', 'all'.

The first stanza owes much of its beauty to the softness and darkness (deep as the colour and perfume of some sleepy dark rose) of the female endings 'sorrow', 'morrow', with their deep vowels and soft 's' and 'm' sinking into languor after the sharper and accented 'joy' and 'night':

There is an end of joy and sorrow;
Peace all day long, all night, all morrow.

The soft female endings are repeated, with the interval of one more poignant line, with a common ending, throughout the stanza. In line four,

'The end is come of pleasant places'

the female ending is less languorous than in the first two lines, because of the alliterative 'pl's' coming so close together. But the fifth line,

'The end of tender words and faces',

sinks again into the same softness, with only the word 'tender' to raise it from its deep languor.

In the second stanza there is an exceedingly beautiful line of alliterative l's:

'No lips to laugh, no lids for tears',

this alliteration giving, for all its softness and deep dark colour, for all its absence of sharp vowels, a great poignance. This effect of poignance may come, in part, from the fact that the soft 'l's' lengthen the line, though almost imperceptibly—in part from the assonance of 'lips' and 'lids'—the word 'lids' being shallower in sound than 'lips'. The extra and disturbed depth and length of the fifth stanza—that beginning with the lines

Wind wherein seas and stars are shaken

Shall shake them, and they shall not waken;

come from the alliterative 's's' and 'sh's'. But a feeling of equilibrium is given by the balanced 'w's' in the first and second words of the first line, and the last word of the second line.

Much of the beauty of this poem comes from Swinburne's power over alliteration, this giving the lines their supreme balance, giving them an added poignance, as in

The grave's mouth laughs unto derision

Desire and dread and dream and vision,

Delight of heaven and sorrow of hell.

The beauty comes in part from this, in part from his amazing power for lengthening a line slightly by using the same letters internally in consecutive words and then outwardly in the word following, as in this line

'The pale old lips of death are fed'

or of lengthening it, more slightly, by using a letter internally in one word and then externally in the next, as in the line

'The breathing flame's mouth curls and kisses'.

Once he causes the line to dip, slightly and sadly, as one bending under the weight of dust, by the device of using, in the middle and again at the end of the line, double-syllabled words in which the second syllable dies away:

'A little sorrow, a little pleasure'.

The second syllable of 'sorrow' is shorter than that of the second syllable of 'pleasure', and it is this subtle change, or difference, and the difference in vowel sounds (the vowel sounds in 'sorrow' being rich, whilst the second vowel sound in 'pleasure' is neutral) which produces this dipping movement.

His use of assonances and dissonances, interspersed with alliteration, is instinctive and inspired. Take, for instance, this stanza, one of the most beautiful in the whole poem:

> [1]'In [2]deep [3]wet ways by [4]grey [5]old [6]gardens
>
> [2]Fed with [5]sharp spring the [1]sweet fruit [5]hardens;
>
> [3]They [4]know not what [3]fruits wane or [4]grow;
>
> [2]Red [6]summer [6½]burns to the [6]utmost [4]ember; [2]
>
> [3]They [4]know not, neither can [2]remember,
>
> [4]The old [6½]years and flowers [3]they used to [4]know.'

The alliteration and the half-tones; these, with the change from the poignant 'e's' to the dulled, the piteous attempt of the sound to lift itself by means of the 'a's' and 'ge's' in the first line, the depth and mournfulness of the 'o' sounds— the effect of these is beautiful, subtle, and strange.

In the poem 'August' the feeling of the roundness and the ripeness of the fruit on the lovely apple-tree, of the dew, of the green leaves, is conveyed, very largely, by the roundness and ripeness of the vowels used.

The word 'gold' is a kind of keynote throughout the poem. In 'August' as in all the finest works of this great poet, there are the faintest stirrings and blood-beats, produced, sometimes, by the repeated use of the same vowel with different vibration-lengths, at other moments by the

use of the same consonant ending two consecutive words.
Take, for instance, this stanza:

> There were four apples on the tree,
> Red stained through gold, that all might see
> The sun went warm from core to rind;
> The green leaves made the summer blind
> In that soft place they kept for me
> With golden apples shut behind.

Now in this verse, the first, and the last two, lines seem to
me to be, very faintly, quicker, seem to be, very faintly,
shorter (though in actuality they are not) than the other
lines. This is due to the fact that the use of the 'd's' in 'red
stained through gold' seems like a prolonging or a deepen-
ing of the colour, whilst there are four consonants together,
d, t, h, r, none of which soar; they are on a level of sound,
and this loss of movement makes the sound seem longer.
Again, the use of the alliterative 'e's' in 'The green leaves'
deepens the sound.

But the whole poem is of an incredible subtlety. The
wandering from the dark to the fuller 'u' sounds, and from
these to the warmer, darker depths of the varying 'o' sounds,
these give a sense of the change to the roundness, warmth
and ripeness of the fruit, after the sharpness of the leaves.
These effects could only have been produced by one of the
greatest artists in his medium.

Here is one example:

> In the mute August afternoon
> They trembled to some undertune
> Of music in the silver air;
> Great pleasure was it to be there
> Till green turned duskier and the moon
> Coloured the corn-sheaves like gold hair.

There is a slight slowing produced by the 'r's' in 'silver air'.

Two stanzas after this, the 'moon', 'noon', 'tune' sounds
are repeated, with fresh subtleties of 'o' sounds.

In this stanza,

> I lay there till the warm smell grew
> More sharp, when flecks of yellow dew
> Between the round ripe leaves had blurred
> The rind with stain and wet; I heard
> A wind that blew and breathed and blew,
> Too weak to alter its one word.

the slight lengthening caused by the 'm's', in 'warm' and
'smell', the pause after 'sharp', the faint difference, so faint
as to be almost imperceptible, between the sounds of 'grew'
and 'dew', of 'blurred' and 'heard', the movement caused
by the different 'e's' in

> A wind that blew and breathed and blew,
> Too weak to alter its one word—

all these subtleties give a feeling of dew falling on those
round ripe leaves, sometimes chilled by a passing air, sometimes not. And this is not only a matter of association,
though association plays its part in the magic, as well as
texture.

In the 1st and 2nd volumes of *Poems and Ballads* and in
'Chastelard' and 'Locrine', exquisite songs are interspersed,
coming to us as 'naked ear-delighting absolute melody—
melody that is just Melody and nothing else; that glides into
the ear, one knows not why . . . that sounds sad when we
are merry and merry when we are sad . . .' This Wagner
wrote, of a different subject. [Posthumous Works.]

Sometimes the songs are too extended, are more beautiful
if they remain in one's ears as fragments only—as this lovely
excerpt from 'Anima Anceps':

> Till death have broken
> Sweet life's love-token,

Till all be spoken
　　That shall be said,
What dost thou praying,
O soul, and playing
With song and saying,
　　Things flown and fled
For this we know not—
That fresh springs flow not
And fresh griefs grow not
　　When men are dead;
When strange years cover
Lover and lover,
And joys are over
　　And tears are shed.

or as the first two verses of 'A Match'.

The poem has no particular meaning; it is just an exquisite sound, like the song of a bird:

If love were what the rose is,
　　And I were like the leaf,
Our lives would grow together
In sad or singing weather,
Blown fields or flowerful closes,
　　Green pleasures or grey grief;
If love were what the rose is,
　　And I were like the leaf.

If I were what the words are,
　　And love were like the tune,
With double sound and single
Delight our lips would mingle,
With kisses glad as birds are
　　That get sweet rain at noon;
If I were what the words are
　　And love were like the tune.

Here, in verse one, by separating the line-end 'roses' from its ryhme 'closes', by one extra line, he avoids the unfortunate sound of the opening lines of 'A Ballad of Dreamland'.

As an example of the over-extension to which the songs are liable, we may take the third and fourth verses of Mary Beaton's song from 'Chastelard':

I.

Between the sunset and the sea
My love laid hands and lips on me;
Of sweet came sour, of day came night,
Of long desire came brief delight:
Ah love, and what thing came of thee
Between the sea-downs and the sea.

II.

Between the sea-mark and the sea
Joy grew to grief, grief grew to me;
Love turned to tears, and tears to fire,
And dead delight to new desire;
Love's talk, love's touch there seemed to be
Between the sea-sand and the sea.

These two verses are exquisite, and the poem would have been more so had the last two been omitted: this may be said especially of Verse III.

III.

Between the sundown and the sea
Love watched one hour of love with me;
Then down the all-golden water-ways
His feet flew after yesterdays;
I saw them come and saw them flee
Between the sea-foam and the sea.

IV.

Between the sea-strand and the sea
Love fell on sleep, sleep fell on me;
The first star saw twain turn to one
Between the moonrise and the sun;
The next, that saw not love, saw me
Between the sea-banks and the sea.

The Ballads in the third Volume of *Poems and Ballads*
contain superb lines, such as these from 'The Weary
Wedding' (although the refrain 'One with another' is,
I think, a mistake and meaningless):

'And what will ye give your sister Jean?
    One with another?'
'A bier to build and a babe to wean,
    Mother, my mother.'

'And what will ye give your sister Nell?
    One with another?'
'The end of life and beginning of hell,
    Mother, my mother.'

.   .   .   .   .   .

'And what will ye give your brother Hugh?
    One with another?'
'A bed of turf to turn into,
    Mother, my mother.'

'And what will ye give your brother John?
    One with another?'
'The dust of death to feed upon,
    Mother, my mother.'

Swinburne's true grandeurs appeared for the first time with
'Atalanta in Calydon', were continued in the First Volume
of *Poems and Ballads*, and certain poems in the second and
third Volumes. After these, his work became, often, misty
and diffuse.

To speak for a moment of the personal life of this great poet and most unhappy man.

His nature had been twisted as a boy at Eton by a horrible sadistic tutor, and to this man, and to Swinburne's addiction to the works of de Sade we must ascribe such poetic falls from grace as 'Hermaphroditus' and 'Dolores'.

Swinburne told Richard Monckton Milnes: '. . . I have known him [the tutor] prepare the flogging-room (not with *corduroy* or *onion*) but with burnt scents; or choose a *sweet* place out of doors with smell of firwood. *This* I call real delicate torment. . . . Once, before giving me a swishing that I had the marks of for more than a month . . . he let me saturate my face with eau-de-Cologne. I conjecture now, on looking back to that "rosy hour", "purged by the euphrosy and rue" of the Marquis de Sade and his philo-sophy, that, counting on the pungency of the perfume and its power over the nerves, he meant to stimulate and excite the senses by that preliminary pleasure so as to inflict the acuter pain afterwards on that awakened and intensified susceptibility.'

In spite of that twisting, his remained, fundamentally, a most noble nature. As Mr Pound wrote of him '. . . there is, underneath all the writing, a magnificent passion for liberty . . . the passion not merely for political, but also for personal liberty is the bedrock of Swinburne's writing. The sense of tragedy, and of the unreasoning cruelty of the gods, hangs over it. He fell into facile writing and he accepted a facile compromise for life; but no facile solution for his universe. His belief did not desert him; no, not even in Putney.'

His was a strange duality of character. On being told by his friend Lady Trevelyan that he was being attacked, on the score of his personal morality, he wrote, 'I cannot express the horror and astonishment, the unutterable indig-nation and loathing, with which I have been struck on hearing that anyone could be vile enough to tax me, I do not say with doing, but with saying anything of the kind to which you refer. The one suggestion is not falser than the other. I am literally amazed and horror-stricken at the infamous wickedness of people who invent in malice or repeat in levity such horrors.

'I cannot believe such persons can really or seriously injure those who are conscious of no wrong done to them which might explain their enmity. It is I who should be ashamed to meet and disgraced by meeting people capable of believing me improper to meet. I can only imagine . . . that as you say I must have talked very foolishly to make such infamies possible; all I can ever recollect saying which *could* be perverted was (for instance) that "the Greeks did not seem to be worse than the moderns because of things considered innocent at one time by one country were not considered so by others". Far more than this I have heard said by men of the highest character. This sort of thing, I was told afterwards, might be thought *wild* and offensive by hearers who were bent on malignant commentary, or . . . I do remember saying if people read the classics, not to speak of the moderns very often, they must see that many qualities called virtues and vices depend on time, climate, and temperament. The remark may have been false or foolish, but who could have imagined it (until he had proof) capable of being twisted into an avowal that I approved vice and disapproved virtue? Anyone who says he has heard me speak personally as if I agreed with other times, or disagreed with this, lies.'

I cannot believe this extremely brave man was a hypocrite.

When Lady Trevelyan was lying on her death-bed, a few hours before her end, she asked John Ruskin (who repeated this in a letter to Edward Coleridge) 'very anxiously what I thought of Swinburne and what he was likely to do and to be. And I answered that she need not be in pain about him—the abuse she heard of him was dreadful, but not, in the deep sense, *moral* evil at all, but mentally physical and ungovernable by his will—and that, finally, God never made such good fruit of human work, to grow on an evil tree.'

Ruskin wrote, a few days later, to Admiral Swinburne, 'You ought not—none of us ought—to be pained grievously by anything in these poems [the First Series of *Poems and Ballads*]. 'The common world cannot distinguish between Coreggio's *Antiope* and a Parisian street lithograph, and mistakes—Carlyle said this long ago—the ill-cut serpent of Eternity for a common poisonous reptile.'

'One might almost pity', Swinburne wrote of Blake, 'the poor age and the poor men he came among for having such a fiery energy cast unawares into the midst of their small customs and competitions.'

It is in Swinburne's book on Blake (of which a gentle-man named J. R. Green—'*mais où sont les nièges d'antan*'—wrote, in *The Saturday Review*, February 1868, that it revealed Swinburne's 'frivolous incapacity as a critic, either of poetry or of art; his inability to think consecutively for five minutes together; his powerlessness to express even his gleams of momentary intelligence in intelligible speech') that we may see Swinburne's true nature.

It is my firm belief that Swinburne, for all his defiance, for all his raging blasphemies, was born a believer. It was his tragedy that he dreamed mankind had been abandoned.

The furies and bitter, fiery tears of certain of the choruses in 'Atalanta', the grey hopelessness of 'At the Foot of the Crucifix', are the result, not of unbelief, but of what he felt was a betrayed faith. This, had it not been for the last deplor-able verses (although I think these have been misunderstood, since it was not against the murdered Christ that he railed, but against those who still betray Him with a kiss, though the last verses contain one unforgivable phrase) would have been a great poem:

Lines from
'Before a Crucifix'

Here, down between the dusty trees,
   At this lank edge of haggard wood,
Women with labour-loosened knees,
   With gaunt backs bowed by servitude,
Stop, shift their loads, and pray, and fare
Forth with souls easier for the prayer.

The suns have branded black, the rains
   Striped grey this piteous God of theirs;
The face is full of prayers and pains,
   To which they bring their pains and prayers;
Lean limbs that show the labouring bones,
And ghastly mouth that gapes and groans.

God of this grievous people, wrought
   After the likeness of their race,
By faces like thine own besought,
   Thine own blind helpless eyeless face,
I, too, that have not tongue nor knee
For prayer, I have a word to thee.

   .   .   .   .   .   .

With iron for thy linen bands
   And unclean cloths for winding-sheet
They bind the people's nail-pierced hands,
   They hide the people's nail-pierced feet;
And what man or what angel known
Shall roll back the sepulchral stone?

But these have not the rich man's grave
   To sleep in when their pain is done.
These were not fit for God to save.
   As naked hell-fire is the sun

In their eyes living, and when dead
These have not where to lay their head.

They have no tomb to dig, and hide;
  Earth is not theirs, that they should sleep.
On all these tombless crucified
  No lovers' eyes have time to weep.
So still, for all man's tears and creeds,
The sacred body hangs and bleeds.

Through the left hand a nail is driven,
  Faith, and another through the right,
Forged in the fires of hell and heaven,
  Fear that puts out the eye of light:
And the feet soiled and scarred and pale
Are pierced with falsehood for a nail.

    .   .   .   .   .   .

O sacred head, O desecrate,
  O labour-wounded feet and hands,
O blood poured forth in pledge to fate
  Of nameless lives in divers lands,
O slain and spent and sacrificed
People, the grey-grown speechless Christ!

Swinburne detested what he described as a 'form of bastard
belief (a) cross-bred between faith and unfaith, which has
been fostered in ages of doubt; a ghost raised rather by fear
than love; by fear of a dead God as judge rather than by
love of a dead God as comforter'.

That 'bastard belief' was not for him. But in 1874, after
John Tyndall's Inaugural Address to the British Association for the Advancement of Science on the relations between science and theology, Swinburne wrote, '. . . science
so enlarged and harmonized gives me a sense as much of

rest as of light. No mythology can make its believers feel less afraid or loth to be reabsorbed into the immeasurable harmony with but the change of a single individual note in a single bar of the tune, than does the faintest perception of the lowest chord touched in the whole system of things. Even my technical ignorance does not impair, I think, my power to see accurately and seize firmly the first thread of the great clue, because my habit of mind is not (I hope) unscientific, though my work lies in the field of art instead of science; and when seen and seized even that first perception gives me an indescribable sense as of music and repose. It is Theism which to me seems to introduce an element—happily a fictitious element—of doubt, discord, and disorder.'

The editor of Swinburne's letters, Mr Cecil Y. Lang, wrote, 'It is not entirely certain that the headstrong, impetuous, self-conscious rebel of the early and middle sixties conceded to Christ the same reverence that, before all other poets, he offered so willingly and humbly to sages, great ethical teachers, or merely elderly men of his own time, but it is clear that thereafter his attitude, within these narrow confines, was not merely decorous but exemplary. "Ever since I knew him", he wrote to his sister in June 1903, referring to Mazzini, "I have been able to read the Gospels with such power of realizing and feeling the truth of the human character of Christ as I have never felt before".'

As he said of Blake, 'His faith was absolute and hard, like a pure fanatic's; there was no speculation in him. What could be made of such a man fed and clothed with the teapot pieties of Cowper and the tape-yard infidelities of Paine? Neither set would have to do with him; was he not a believer? And was he not a blasphemer? His licence of thought and talk was always of the maddest, or seemed so to the ears of his generation. . . . Now on his own ground, no man was ever more sane or more reverent. His outcries on various matters of art or morals were in effect the mere expression, not of reasonable dissent, but of violent belief. . . . Indifference was impossible to him.'

Swinburne lived after the time of Cowper—in an age of worse poetry than Cowper's 'teapot-pieties'—but that noble passage from his book on William Blake might have been his own epitaph.

A BALLAD OF LIFE

I found in dreams a place of wind and flowers,
  Full of sweet trees and colour of glad grass,
  In midst whereof there was
A lady clothed like summer with sweet hours;
Her beauty, fervent as a fiery moon,
  Made my blood burn and swoon
    Like a flame rained upon.
Sorrow had filled her shaken eyelids' blue,
And her mouth's sad red heavy rose all through
  Seemed sad with glad things gone.

She held a little cithern by the strings,
  Shaped heartwise, strung with subtle-coloured hair
  Of some dead lute player
That in dead years had done delicious things.
The seven strings were named accordingly;
  The first string charity,
    The second tenderness,
The rest were pleasure, sorrow, sleep, and sin,
And loving kindness, that is pity's kin
  And is most pitiless.

There were three men with her, each garmented
  With gold and shod with gold upon the feet,
  And with plucked ears of wheat.
The first man's hair was wound upon his head:

53

His face was red, and his mouth curled and sad;
   All his gold garment had
      Pale stains of dust and rust.
A riven hood was pulled across his eyes;
The token of him being upon this wise
      Made for a sign of Lust.

The next was Shame, with hollow heavy face
   Coloured like green wood when flame kindles it.
   He hath such feeble feet
They may not well endure in any place.
His face was full of grey old miseries,
   And all his blood's increase
      Was even increase of pain.
The last was Fear, that is akin to Death;
He is Shame's friend, and always as Shame saith
   Fear answers him again.

My soul said in me: This is marvellous,
   Seeing the air's face is not so delicate
   Nor the sun's grace so great,
If sin and she be kin or amorous.
And seeing where maidens served her on their knees,
   I bade one crave of these
      To know the cause thereof.
Then Fear said: I am Pity that was dead.
And Shame said: I am Sorrow comforted.
   And Lust said: I am Love.

Thereat her hands began a lute-playing
   And her sweet mouth a song in a strange tongue;
   And all the while she sung
There was no sound but long tears following

Long tears upon men's faces, waxen white
  With extreme sad delight.
    But those three following men
Became as men raised up among the dead;
Great glad mouths open, and fair cheeks made red
  With child's blood come again.

Then I said: Now assuredly I see
  My lady is perfect, and transfigureth
  All sin and sorrow and death,
Making them fair as her own eyelids be,
Or lips wherein my whole soul's life abides;
  Or as her sweet white sides
    And bosom carved to kiss.
Now therefore, if her pity further me,
Doubtless for her sake all my days shall be
  As righteous as she is.

Forth, ballad, and take roses in both arms,
  Even till the top rose touch thee in the throat
Where the least thornprick harms;
  And girdled in thy golden singing-coat,
Come thou before my lady and say this;
  Borgia, thy gold hair's colour burns in me,
    Thy mouth makes beat my blood in feverish rhymes;
Therefore so many as these roses be,
  Kiss me so many times.
Then it may be, seeing how sweet she is,
  That she will stoop herself none otherwise
  Than a blown vine-branch doth,
And kiss thee with soft laughter on thine eyes,
  Ballad, and on thy mouth.

A BALLAD OF DEATH

Kneel down, fair Love, and fill thyself with tears,
Girdle thyself with sighing for a girth
Upon the sides of mirth,
Cover thy lips and eyelids, let thine ears
Be filled with rumour of people sorrowing;
Make thee soft raiment out of woven sighs
Upon the flesh to cleave,
Set pains therein and many a grievous thing,
And many sorrows after each his wise,
For armlet and for gorget and for sleeve.

O Love's lute heard about the lands of death,
Left hanged upon the trees that were therein;
O Love and Time and Sin,
Three singing mouths that mourn now under breath,
Three lovers, each one evil spoken of;
O smitten lips wherethrough this voice of mine
Came softer with her praise;
Abide a little for our lady's love.
The kisses of her mouth were more than wine,
And more than peace the passage of her days.

O Love, thou knowest if she were good to see.
O Time, thou shalt not find in any land
Till, cast out of thine hand,
The sunlight and the moonlight fail from thee,

Another woman fashioned like as this.
O Sin, thou knowest that all thy shame in her
Was made a goodly thing;
Yea, she caught Shame and shamed him with her kiss,
With her fair kiss, and lips much lovelier
Than lips of amorous roses in late spring.

By night there stood over against my bed
Queen Venus with a hood striped gold and black,
Both sides drawn fully back
From brows wherein the sad blood failed of red,
And temples drained of purple and full of death.
Her curled hair had the wave of sea-water
And the sea's gold in it.
Her eyes were as a dove's that sickeneth.
Strewn dust of gold she had shed over her,
And pearl and purple and amber on her feet.

Upon her raiment of dyed sendaline
Were painted all the secret ways of love
And covered things thereof,
That hold delight as grape-flowers hold their wine;
Red mouths of maidens and red feet of doves,
And brides that kept within the bride-chamber
Their garment of soft shame,
And weeping faces of the wearied loves
That swoon in sleep and awake wearier,
With heat of lips and hair shed out like flame.

The tears that through her eyelids fell on me
Made mine own bitter where they ran between
As blood had fallen therein,
She saying; Arise, lift up thine eyes and see

E   57

If any glad thing be or any good
Now the best thing is taken forth of us;
Even she to whom all praise
Was as one flower in a great multitude,
One glorious flower of many and glorious,
One day found gracious among many days:

Even she whose handmaiden was Love—to whom
At kissing times across her stateliest bed
Kings bowed themselves and shed
Pale wine, and honey with the honeycomb,
And spikenard bruised for a burnt-offering;
Even she between whose lips the kiss became
As fire and frankincense;
Whose hair was as gold raiment on a king,
Whose eyes were as the morning purged with flame,
Whose eyelids as sweet savour issuing thence.

Then I beheld, and lo on the other side
My lady's likeness crowned and robed and dead.
Sweet still, but now not red,
Was the shut mouth whereby men lived and died.
And sweet, but emptied of the blood's blue shade,
The great curled eyelids that withheld her eyes.
And sweet, but like spoilt gold,
The weight of colour in her tresses weighed.
And sweet, but as a vesture with new dyes,
The body that was clothed with love of old.

Ah! that my tears filled all her woven hair
And all the hollow bosom of her gown—
Ah! that my tears ran down
Even to the place where many kisses were,

58

Even where her parted breast-flowers have place,
Even where they are cloven apart—who knows not this?
Ah! the flowers cleave apart
And their sweet fills the tender interspace;
Ah! the leaves grown thereof were things to kiss
Ere their fine gold was tarnished at the heart.

Ah! in the days when God did good to me,
Each part about her was a righteous thing;
Her mouth an almsgiving,
The glory of her garments charity,
The beauty of her bosom a good deed,
In the good days when God kept sight of us;
Love lay upon her eyes,
And on that hair whereof the world takes heed:
And all her body was more virtuous
Than souls of women fashioned otherwise.

Now, ballad, gather poppies in thine hands
And sheaves of brier and many rusted sheaves
Rain-rotten in rank lands,
Waste marigold and late unhappy leaves
And grass that fades ere any of it be mown;
And when thy bosom is filled full thereof
Seek out Death's face ere the light altereth,
And say 'My master that was thrall to Love
Is become thrall to Death.'
Bow down before him, ballad, sigh and groan,
But make no sojourn in thy outgoing;
For haply it may be
That when thy feet return at evening
Death shall come in with thee.

LAUS VENERIS

Asleep or waking is it? for her neck,
Kissed over close, wears yet a purple speck
   Wherein the pained blood falters and goes out;
Soft, and stung softly—fairer for a fleck.

But though my lips shut sucking on the place,
There is no vein at work upon her face;
   Her eyelids are so peaceable, no doubt
Deep sleep has warmed her blood through all its ways.

Lo, this is she that was the world's delight;
The old grey years were parcels of her might;
   The strewings of the ways wherein she trod
Were the twain seasons of the day and night.

Lo, she was thus when her clear limbs enticed
All lips that now grow sad with kissing Christ,
   Stained with blood fallen from the feet of God,
The feet and hands whereat our souls were priced.

Alas, Lord, surely thou art great and fair.
But lo her wonderfully woven hair!
   And thou didst heal us with thy piteous kiss;
But see now, Lord; her mouth is lovelier.

She is right fair; what hath she done to thee?
Nay, fair Lord Christ, lift up thine eyes and see:
  Had now thy mother such a lip—like this?
Thou knowest how sweet a thing it is to me.

Inside the Horsel here the air is hot;
Right little peace one hath for it, God wot;
  The scented dusty daylight burns the air,
And my heart chokes me till I hear it not.

Behold, my Venus, my soul's body, lies,
With my love laid upon her garment-wise,
  Feeling my love in all her limbs and hair
And shed between her eyelids through her eyes.

She holds my heart in her sweet open hands
Hanging asleep; hard by her head there stands,
  Crowned with gilt thorns and clothed with flesh
                    like fire,
Love, wan as foam blown up the salt burnt sands—

Hot as the brackish waifs of yellow spume
That shift and steam—loose clots of arid fume
  From the sea's panting mouth of dry desire;
There stands he, like one labouring at a loom.

The warp holds fast across; and every thread
That makes the woof up has dry specks of red;
  Always the shuttle cleaves clean through, and he
Weaves with the hair of many a ruined head.

Love is not glad nor sorry, as I deem;
Labouring he dreams, and labours in the dream,
    Till when the spool is finished, lo I see
His web, reeled off, curls and goes out like steam.

Night falls like fire; the heavy lights run low,
And as they drop, my blood and body so
    Shake as the flame shakes, full of days and hours
That sleep not neither weep they as they go.

Ah yet would God this flesh of mine might be
Where air might wash and long leaves cover me,
    Where tides of grass break into foam of flowers,
Or where the wind's feet shine along the sea.

Ah yet would God that stems and roots were bred
Out of my weary body and my head,
    That sleep were sealed upon me with a seal,
And I were as the least of all his dead.

Would God my blood were dew to feed the grass,
Mine ears made deaf and mine eyes blind as glass,
    My body broken as a turning wheel,
And my mouth stricken ere it saith Alas!

Ah God, that love were as a flower or flame,
That life were as the naming of a name,
    That death were not more pitiful than desire,
That these things were not one thing and the same!

Behold now, surely somewhere there is death:
For each man hath some space of years, he saith,
    A little space of time ere time expire,
A little day, a little way of breath.

And lo, between the sundawn and the sun,
His day's work and his night's work are undone;
 And lo, between the nightfall and the light,
He is not, and none knoweth of such an one.

Ah God, that I were as all souls that be,
As any herb or leaf of any tree,
 As men that toil through hours of labouring night,
As bones of men under the deep sharp sea.

Outside it must be winter among men;
For at the gold bars of the gates again
 I heard all night and all the hours of it,
The wind's wet wings and fingers drip with rain.

Knights gather, riding sharp for cold; I know
The ways and woods are strangled with the snow;
 And with short song the maidens spin and sit
Until Christ's birthnight, lily-like, arow.

The scent and shadow shed about me make
The very soul in all my senses ache;
 The hot hard night is fed upon my breath,
And sleep beholds me from afar awake.

Alas, but surely where the hills grow deep,
Or where the wild ways of the sea are steep,
 Or in strange places somewhere there is death,
And on death's face the scattered hair of sleep.

There lover-like with lips and limbs that meet
They lie, they pluck sweet fruit of life and eat;
 But me the hot and hungry days devour,
And in my mouth no fruit of theirs is sweet.

No fruit of theirs, but fruit of my desire,
For her love's sake whose lips through mine respire;
   Her eyelids on her eyes like flower on flower,
Mine eyelids on mine eyes like fire on fire.

So lie we, not as sleep that lies by death,
With heavy kisses and with happy breath;
   Not as man lies by woman, when the bride
Laughs low for love's sake and the words he saith.

For she lies, laughing low with love; she lies
And turns his kisses on her lips to sighs,
   To sighing sound of lips unsatisfied,
And the sweet tears are tender with her eyes.

Ah, not as they, but as the souls that were
Slain in the old time, having found her fair;
   Who, sleeping with her lips upon their eyes,
Heard sudden serpents hiss across her hair.

Their blood runs round the roots of time like rain:
She casts them forth and gathers them again;
   With nerve and bone she weaves and multiplies
Exceeding pleasure out of extreme pain.

Her little chambers drip with flower-like red,
Her girdles, and the chaplets of her head,
   Her armlets and her anklets; with her feet
She tramples all that winepress of the dead.

Her gateways smoke with fume of flowers and fires,
With loves burnt out and unassuaged desires;
   Between her lips the steam of them is sweet,
The languor in her ears of many lyres.

Her beds are full of perfume and sad sound,
Her doors are made with music, and barred round
   With sighing and with laughter and with tears,
With tears whereby strong souls of men are bound.

There is the knight Adonis that was slain,
With flesh and blood she chains him for a chain;
   The body and the spirit in her ears
Cry, for her lips divide him vein by vein.

Yea, all she slayeth; yea, every man save me;
Me, love, thy lover that must cleave to thee
   Till the ending of the days and ways of earth,
The shaking of the sources of the sea.

Me, most forsaken of all souls that fell;
Me, satiated with things insatiable;
   Me, for whose sake the extreme hell makes mirth,
Yea, laughter kindles at the heart of hell.

Alas thy beauty! for thy mouth's sweet sake
My soul is bitter to me, my limbs quake
   As water, as the flesh of men that weep,
As their heart's vein whose heart goes nigh to break.

Ah God, that sleep with flower-sweet finger-tips
Would crush the fruit of death upon my lips;
   Ah God, that death would tread the grapes of sleep
And wring their juice upon me as it drips.

There is no change of cheer for many days,
But change of chimes high up in the air, that sways
   Rung by the running fingers of the wind;
And singing sorrows heard on hidden ways.

Day smiteth day in twain, night sundereth night,
And on mine eyes the dark sits as the light;
 Yea, Lord, thou knowest I know not, having sinned,
If heaven be clean or unclean in thy sight.

Yea, as if earth were sprinkled over me,
Such chafed harsh earth as chokes a sandy sea,
 Each pore doth yearn, and the dried blood thereof
Gasps by sick fits, my heart swims heavily,

There is a feverish famine in my veins;
Below her bosom, where a crushed grape stains
 The white and blue, there my lips caught and clove
An hour since, and what mark of me remains?

I dare not always touch her, lest the kiss
Leave my lips charred. Yea, Lord, a little bliss,
 Brief bitter bliss, one hath for a great sin;
Nathless thou knowest how sweet a thing it is.

Sin, is it sin whereby men's souls are thrust
Into the pit? yet had I a good trust
 To save my soul before it slipped therein,
Trod under by the fire-shod feet of lust.

For if mine eyes fail and my soul takes breath,
I look between the iron sides of death
 Into sad hell where all sweet love hath end,
All but the pain that never finisheth.

There are the naked faces of great kings,
The singing folk with all their lute-playings;
 There when one cometh he shall have to friend
The grave that covets and the worm that clings.

There sit the knights that were so great of hand,
The ladies that were queens of fair green land,
   Grown grey and black now, brought unto the dust,
Soiled, without raiment, clad about with sand.

There is one end for all of them; they sit
Naked and sad, they drink the dregs of it,
   Trodden as grapes in the wine-press of lust,
Trampled and trodden by the fiery feet.

I see the marvellous mouth whereby there fell
Cities and people whom the gods loved well,
   Yet for her sake on them the fire gat hold,
And for their sakes on her the fire of hell.

And softer than the Egyptian lote-leaf is,
The queen whose face was worth the world to kiss,
   Wearing at breast a suckling snake of gold;
And large pale lips of strong Semiramis,

Curled like a tiger's that curl back to feed;
Red only where the last kiss made them bleed;
   Her hair most thick with many a carven gem,
Deep in the mane, great-chested, like a steed.

Yea, with red sin the faces of them shine;
But in all these there was no sin like mine;
   No, not in all the strange great sins of them
That made the wine-press froth and foam with wine.

For I was of Christ's choosing, I God's knight,
No blinkard heathen stumbling for scant light;
   I can well see, for all the dusty days
Gone past, the clean great time of goodly fight.

I smell the breathing battle sharp with blows,
With shriek of shafts and snapping short of bows;
   The fair pure sword smites out in subtle ways,
Sounds and long lights are shed between the rows

Of beautiful mailed men; the edged light slips,
Most like a snake that takes short breath and dips
   Sharp from the beautifully bending head,
With all its gracious body lithe as lips

That curl in touching you; right in this wise
My sword doth, seeming fire in mine own eyes,
   Leaving all colours in them brown and red
And flecked with death; then the keen breaths like sighs,

The caught-up choked dry laughters following them,
When all the fighting face is grown a flame
   For pleasure, and the pulse that stuns the ears,
And the heart's gladness of the goodly game.

Let me think yet a little; I do know
These things were sweet, but sweet such years ago,
   Their savour is all turned now into tears:
Yea, ten years since, where the blue ripples blow

The blue curled eddies of the blowing Rhine,
I felt the sharp wind shaking grass and vine
   Touch my blood too, and sting me with delight
Through all this waste and weary body of mine

That never feels clear air; right gladly then
I rode alone, a great way off my men,
   And heard the chiming bridle smite and smite,
And gave each rhyme thereof some rhyme again,

Till my song shifted to that iron one;
Seeing there rode up between me and the sun
   Some certain of my foe's men, for his three
White wolves across their painted coats did run.

The first red-bearded, with square cheeks—alack,
I made my knave's blood turn his beard to black;
   The slaying of him was a joy to see:
Perchance too, when at night he came not back,

Some woman fell a-weeping, whom this thief
Would beat when he had drunken; yet small grief
   Hath any for the ridding of such knaves;
Yea, if one wept, I doubt her teen was brief.

This bitter love is sorrow in all lands,
Draining of eyelids, wringing of drenched hands,
   Sighing of hearts and filling up of graves;
A sign across the head of the world he stands,

As one that hath a plague-mark on his brows;
Dust and spilt blood do track him to his house
   Down under earth; sweet smells of lip and cheek
Like a sweet snake's breath made more poisonous

With chewing of some perfumed deadly grass,
Are shed all round his passage if he pass,
   And their quenched savour leaves the whole soul weak.
Sick with keen guessing whence the perfume was.

As one who hidden in deep sedge and reeds
Smells the rare scent made where a panther feeds,
   And tracking ever slotwise the warm smell
Is snapped upon by the sweet mouth and bleeds,

69

His head far down the hot sweet throat of her—
So one tracks love, whose breath is deadlier,
 And lo, one springe and you are fast in hell,
Fast as the gin's grip of a wayfarer.

I think now, as the heavy hours decease
One after one, and bitter thoughts increase
 One upon one, of all sweet finished things;
The breaking of the battle; the long peace

Wherein we sat clothed softly, each man's hair
Crowned with green leaves beneath white hoods of vair;
 The sounds of sharp spears at great tourneyings,
And noise of singing in the late sweet air.

I sang of love, too, knowing nought thereof;
'Sweeter', I said, 'the little laugh of love
 Than tears out of the eyes of Magdalen,
Or any fallen feather of the Dove.

'The broken little laugh that spoils a kiss,
The ache of purple pulses, and the bliss
 Of blinded eyelids that expand again—
Love draws them open with those lips of his,

'Lips that cling hard till the kissed face has grown
Of one same fire and colour with their own;
 Then ere one sleep, appeased with sacrifice,
Where his lips wounded, there his lips atone.'

I sang these things long since and knew them not;
'Lo, here is love, or there is love, God wot,
 This man and that finds favour in his eyes,'
I said, 'but I, what guerdon have I got?'

70

'The dust of praise that is blown everywhere
In all men's faces with the common air;
   The bay-leaf that wants chafing to be sweet
Before they wind it in a singer's hair.'

So that one dawn I rode forth sorrowing;
I had no hope but of some evil thing,
   And so rode slowly past the windy wheat
And past the vineyard and the water-spring.

Up to the Horsel. A great elder-tree
Held back its heaps of flowers to let me see
   The ripe tall grass, and one that walked therein,
Naked, with hair shed over to the knee.

She walked between the blossom and the grass;
I knew the beauty of her, what she was,
   The beauty of her body and her sin,
And in my flesh the sin of hers, alas!

Alas! for sorrow is all the end of this.
O sad kissed mouth, how sorrowful it is!
   O breast whereat some suckling sorrow clings,
Red with the bitter blossom of a kiss!

Ah, with blind lips I felt for you, and found
About my neck your hands and hair enwound,
   The hands that stifle and the hair that stings,
I felt them fasten sharply without sound.

Yea, for my sin I had great store of bliss:
Rise up, make answer for me, let thy kiss
   Seal my lips hard from speaking of my sin,
Lest one go mad to hear how sweet it is.

71

Yet I waxed faint with fume of barren bowers,
And murmuring of the heavy-headed hours;
   And let the dove's beak fret and peck within
My lips in vain, and Love shed fruitless flowers

So that God looked upon me when your hands
Were hot about me; yea, God brake my bands
   To save my soul alive, and I came forth
Like a man blind and naked in strange lands

That hears men laugh and weep, and knows not whence
Nor wherefore, but is broken in his sense;
   Howbeit I met folk riding from the north
Towards Rome, to purge them of their souls' offence.

And rode with them, and spake to none; the day
Stunned me like lights upon some wizard way,
   And ate like fire mine eyes and mine eyesight;
So rode I, hearing all these chant and pray,

And marvelled; till before us rose and fell
White cursed hills, like outer skirts of hell
   Seen where men's eyes look through the day to night,
Like a jagged shell's lips, harsh, untunable,

Blown in between by devils' wrangling breath;
Nathless we won well past that hell and death,
   Down to the sweet land where all airs are good,
Even unto Rome where God's grace tarrieth.

Then came each man and worshipped at his knees
Who in the Lord God's likeness bears the keys
   To bind or loose, and called on Christ's shed blood,
And so the sweet-souled father gave him ease.

But when I came I fell down at his feet,
Saying, 'Father, though the Lord's blood be right sweet,
   The spot it takes not off the panther's skin,
Nor shall an Ethiop's stain be bleached with it.

'Lo, I have sinned and have spat out at God,
Wherefore his hand is heavier and his rod
   More sharp because of mine exceeding sin,
And all his raiment redder than bright blood

'Before mine eyes; yea, for my sake I wot
The heat of hell is waxen seven times hot
   Through my great sin.' Then spake he some
                    sweet word,
Giving me cheer; which thing availed me not.

Yea, scarce I wist if such indeed were said;
For when I ceased—lo, as one newly dead
   Who hears a great cry out of hell, I heard
The crying of his voice across my head.

'Until this dry shred staff, that hath no whit
Of leaf nor bark, bear blossom and smell sweet,
   Seek thou not any mercy in God's sight,
For so long shalt thou be cast out from it.'

Yea, what if dried-up stems wax red and green,
Shall that thing be which is not nor has been?
   Yea, what if sapless bark wax green and white,
Shall any good fruit grow upon my sin?

Nay, though sweet fruit were plucked of a dry tree,
And though men drew sweet waters of the sea,
   There should not grow sweet leaves on this dead stem,
This waste wan body and shaken soul of me.

Yea, though God search it warily enough,
There is not one sound thing in all thereof;
   Though he search all my veins through, searching them
He shall find nothing whole therein but love.

For I came home right heavy, with small cheer,
And lo my love, mine own soul's heart, more dear
   Than mine own soul, more beautiful than God,
Who hath my being between the hands of her—

Fair still, but fair for no man saving me,
As when she came out of the naked sea
   Making the foam as fire whereon she trod,
And as the inner flower of fire was she.

Yea, she laid hold upon me, and her mouth
Clove unto mine as soul to body doth,
   And, laughing, made her lips luxurious;
Her hair had smells of all the sunburnt south.

Strange spice and flower, strange savour of crushed fruit,
And perfume the swart kings tread underfoot
   For pleasure when their minds wax amorous,
Charred frankincense and grated sandal-root.

And I forgot fear and all weary things,
All ended prayers and perished thanksgivings,
   Feeling her face with all her eager hair
Cleave to me, clinging as a fire that clings

To the body and to the raiment, burning them;
As after death I know that such-like flame
   Shall cleave to me for ever; yea, what care,
Albeit I burn then having felt the same?

Ah love, there is no better life than this;
To have known love, how bitter a thing it is,
   And afterward be cast out of God's sight;
Yea, these that know not, shall they have such bliss

High up in barren heaven before his face
As we twain in the heavy-hearted place,
   Remembering love and all the dead delight,
And all that time was sweet with for a space?

For till the thunder in the trumpet be,
Soul may divide from body, but not we
   One from another; I hold thee with my hand,
I let mine eyes have all their will of thee,

I seal myself upon thee with my might,
Abiding alway out of all men's sight
   Until God loosen over sea and land
The thunder of the trumpets of the night.

            Explicit *Laus Veneris*.

TRANSLATIONS FROM THE FRENCH OF VILLON

I

The Complaint of the Fair Armouress

I

Meseemeth I heard cry and groan
    That sweet who was the armourer's maid;
For her young years she made sore moan,
    And right upon this wise she said;
    'Ah fierce old age with foul bald head,
To spoil fair things thou art over fain;
    Who holdeth me? who? would God I were dead!
Would God I were well dead and slain!

II

'Lo, thou hast broken the sweet yoke
    That my high beauty held above
All priests and clerks and merchant-folk;
    There was not one but for my love
    Would give me gold and gold enough,
Though sorrow his very heart had riven,
    To win from me such wage thereof
As now no thief would take if given.

76

III

'I was right chary of the same,
  God wot it was my great folly,
For love of one sly knave of them
  Good store of that same sweet had he;
  For all my subtle wiles, perdie,
God wot I loved him well enow;
  Right evilly he handled me,
But he loved well my gold, I trow.

IV

'Though I gat bruises green and black,
  I loved him never the less a jot;
Though he bound burdens on my back,
  If he said "Kiss me and heed it not"
  Right little pain I felt, God wot,
When that foul thief's mouth, found so sweet,
  Kissed me—Much good thereof I got!
I keep the sin and the shame of it.

V

'And he died thirty year agone.
  I am old now, no sweet thing to see;
By God, though, when I think thereon,
  And of that good glad time, woe's me,
  And stare upon my changed body
Stark naked, that has been so sweet,
  Lean, wizen, like a small dry tree,
I am nigh mad with the pain of it.

VI

'Where is my faultless forehead's white,
  The lifted eyebrows, soft gold hair,
Eyes wide apart and keen of sight,
  With subtle skill in the amorous air;
  The straight nose, great nor small, but fair,
The small carved ears of shapeliest growth,
  Chin dimpling, colour good to wear,
And sweet red splendid kissing mouth?

VII

'The shapely slender shoulders small,
  Long arms, hands wrought in glorious wise,
Round little breasts, the hips withal
  High, full of flesh, not scant of size,
  Fit for all amorous masteries;

  .   .   .   .

  .   .   .   .

  .   .   .   .

VIII

'A writhled forehead, hair gone grey,
  Fallen eyebrows, eyes gone blind and red,
Their laughs and looks all fled away,
  Yea, all that smote men's hearts are fled;
  The bowed nose, fallen from goodlihead;
Foul flapping ears like water-flags;
  Peaked chin, and cheeks all waste and dead,
And lips that are two skinny rags:

78

IX

'Thus endeth all the beauty of us.
  The arms made short, the hands made lean,
The shoulders bowed and ruinous,
  The breasts, alack! all fallen in;
  The flanks too, like the breasts, grown thin;

. . . .

  For the lank thighs, no thighs but skin,
They are specked with spots like sausage-meat.

X

'So we make moan for the old sweet days,
  Poor old light women, two or three
Squatting above the straw-fire's blaze,
  The bosom crushed against the knee,
  Like faggots on a heap we be,
Round fires soon lit, soon quenched and done,
  And we were once so sweet, even we!
Thus fareth many and many an one.'

TRANSLATIONS FROM THE
FRENCH OF VILLON

2

Epistle in form of a Ballad to his Friends

Have pity, pity, friends, have pity on me,
    Thus much at least, may it please you, of your grace!
I lie not under hazel or hawthorn-tree
    Down in this dungeon ditch, mine exile's place
    By leave of God and fortune's foul disgrace.
Girls, lovers, glad young folk and newly wed,
Jumpers and jugglers, tumbling heel o'er head,
    Swift as a dart, and sharp as needle-ware,
Throats clear as bells that ring the kine to shed,
    Your poor old friend, what, will you leave him there?

Singers that sing at pleasure, lawlessly,
    Light, laughing, gay of word and deed, that race
And run like folk light-witted as ye be
    And have in hand nor current coin nor base,
    Ye wait too long, for now he's dying apace.
Rhymers of lays and roundels sung and read,
Ye'll brew him broth too late when he lies dead.
    Nor wind nor lightning, sunbeam nor fresh air,
May pierce the thick wall's bound where lies his bed;
    Your poor old friend, what, will you leave him there?

O noble folk from tithes and taxes free,
  Come and behold him in this piteous case,
Ye that nor king nor emperor holds in fee,
  But only God in heaven; behold his face
  Who needs must fast, Sundays and holidays,
Which makes his teeth like rakes; and when he hath fed
With never a cake for banquet but dry bread,
  Must drench his bowels with much cold watery fare,
With board nor stool, but low on earth instead;
  Your poor old friend, what, will you leave him there?

Princes afore-named, old and young foresaid,
Get me the king's seal and my pardon sped,
  And hoist me in some basket up with care:
So swine will help each other ill bested,
For where one squeaks they run in heaps ahead.
Your poor old friend, what, will you leave him there?

A LEAVE-TAKING

Let us go hence, my songs; she will not hear.
Let us go hence together without fear;
Keep silence now, for singing-time is over,
And over all old things and all things dear.
She loves not you nor me as all we love her.
Yea, though we sang as angels in her ear,
      She would not hear.

Let us rise up and part; she will not know.
Let us go seaward as the great winds go,
Full of blown sand and foam; what help is there?
There is no help, for all these things are so,
And all the world is bitter as a tear.
And how these things are, though ye strove to show
      She would not know.

Let us go home and hence; she will not weep.
We gave love many dreams and days to keep,
Flowers without scent, and fruits that would not grow,
Saying, 'If thou wilt, thrust in thy sickle and reap.'
All is reaped now; no grass is left to mow;
And we that sowed, though all we fell on sleep,
      She would not weep.

Let us go hence and rest; she will not love.
She shall not hear us if we sing hereof,
Nor see love's ways, how sore they are and steep.
Come hence, let be, lie still; it is enough.
Love is a barren sea, bitter and deep;
And though she saw all heaven in flower above,
      She would not love.

Let us give up, go down; she will not care.
Though all the stars made gold of all the air,
And the sea moving saw before it move
One moon-flower making all the foam-flowers fair;
Though all those waves went over us, and drove
Deep down the stifling lips and drowning hair,
      She would not care.

Let us go hence, go hence, she will not see.
Sing all once more together; surely she,
She too, remembering days and words that were,
Will turn a little toward us, sighing; but we,
We are hence, we are gone, as though we had not been
                    there.
Nay, and though all men seeing had pity on me,
      She would not see.

ITYLUS

Swallow, my sister, O sister swallow,
  How can thine heart be full of the spring?
    A thousand summers are over and dead.
What hast thou found in the spring to follow?
  What hast thou found in thine heart to sing?
    What wilt thou do when the summer is shed?

O swallow, sister, O fair swift swallow,
  Why wilt thou fly after spring to the south,
    The soft south whither thine heart is set?
Shall not the grief of the old time follow?
  Shall not the song thereof cleave to thy mouth?
    Hast thou forgotten ere I forget?

Sister, my sister, O fleet sweet swallow,
  Thy way is long to the sun and the south,
    But I, fulfilled of my heart's desire,
Shedding my song upon height, upon hollow,
  From tawny body and sweet small mouth
    Feed the heart of the night with fire.

I the nightingale all spring through,
  O swallow, sister, O changing swallow,
    All spring through till the spring be done,
Clothed with the light of the night on the dew,
  Sing, while the hours and the wild birds follow,
    Take flight and follow and find the sun.

Sister, my sister, O soft light swallow,
  Though all things feast in the spring's guest-chamber,
    How hast thou heart to be glad thereof yet?
For where thou fliest I shall not follow,
  Till life forget and death remember,
    Till thou remember and I forget.

Swallow, my sister, O singing swallow,
  I know not how thou hast heart to sing.
    Hast thou the heart? is it all past over?
Thy lord the summer is good to follow,
  And fair the feet of thy lover the spring:
    But what wilt thou say to the spring thy lover?

O swallow, sister, O fleeting swallow,
  My heart in me is a molten ember
    And over my head the waves have met.
But thou wouldst tarry or I would follow,
  Could I forget or thou remember,
    Couldst thou remember and I forget.

O sweet stray sister, O shifting swallow,
  The heart's division divideth us.
    Thy heart is light as a leaf of a tree;
But mine goes forth among sea-gulfs hollow
  To the place of the slaying of Itylus,
    The feast of Daulis, the Thracian sea.

O swallow, sister, O rapid swallow,
  I pray thee sing not a little space.
    Are not the roofs and the lintels wet?
The woven web that was plain to follow,
  The small slain body, the flower-like face,
    Can I remember if thou forget?

O sister, sister, thy first-begotten!
   The hands that cling and the feet that follow,
      The voice of the child's blood crying yet
Who hath remembered me? who hath forgotten?
   Thou hast forgotten, O summer swallow,
      But the world shall end when I forget.

THE LEPER

Nothing is better, I well think,
   Than love; the hidden well-water
Is not so delicate to drink:
   This was well seen of me and her.

I served her in a royal house;
   I served her wine and curious meat
For will to kiss between her brows
   I had no heart to sleep or eat.

Mere scorn God knows she had of me;
   A poor scribe, nowise great or fair,
Who plucked his clerk's hood back to see
   Her curled-up lips and amorous hair.

I vex my head with thinking this.
   Yea, though God always hated me,
And hates me now that I can kiss
   Her eyes, plait up her hair to see

How she then wore it on the brows,
   Yet am I glad to have her dead
Here in this wretched wattled house
   Where I can kiss her eyes and head.

Nothing is better, I well know,
   Than love; no amber in cold sea
Or gathered berries under snow:
   That is well seen of her and me.

Three thoughts I make my pleasure of:
   First I take heart and think of this:
That knight's gold hair she chose to love,
   His mouth she had such will to kiss.

Then I remember that sundawn
   I brought him by a privy way
Out of her lattice, and thereon
   What gracious words she found to say.

(Cold rushes for such little feet—
   Both feet could lie into my hand.
A marvel was it of my sweet
   Her upright body could so stand.)

'Sweet friend, God give you thank and grace
   Now am I clean and whole of shame,
Nor shall men burn me in the face
   For my sweet fault that scandals them.'

I tell you over word by word.
   She, sitting edgewise on her bed,
Holding her feet, said thus. The third,
   A sweeter thing than these, I said.

God, that makes time and ruins it
   And alters not, abiding God,
Changed with disease her body sweet,
   The body of love wherein she abode.

Love is more sweet and comelier
    Than a dove's throat strained out to sing.
All they spat out and cursed at her
    And cast her forth for a base thing.

They cursed her, seeing how God had wrought
    This curse to plague her, a curse of his.
Fools were they surely, seeing not
    How sweeter than all sweet she is.

He that had held her by the hair,
    With kissing lips blinding her eyes,
Felt her bright bosom, strained and bare,
    Sigh under him, with short mad cries

Out of her throat and sobbing mouth
    And body broken up with love,
With sweet hot tears his lips were loth
    Her own should taste the savour of,

Yea, he inside whose grasp all night
    Her fervent body leapt or lay,
Stained with sharp kisses red and white,
    Found her a plague to spurn away.

I hid her in this wattled house,
    I served her water and poor bread.
For joy to kiss between her brows
    Time upon time I was nigh dead.

Bread failed; we got but well-water
    And gathered grass with dropping seed.
I had such joy of kissing her,
    I had small care to sleep or feed.

Sometimes when service made me glad
    The sharp tears leapt between my lids,
Falling on her, such joy I had
    To do the service God forbids.

'I pray you let me be at peace,
    Get hence, make room for me to die.'
She said that: her poor lip would cease,
    Put up to mine, and turn to cry.

I said, 'Bethink yourself how love
    Fared in us twain, what either did;
Shall I unclothe my soul thereof?
    That I should do this, God forbid.'

Yea, though God hateth us, he knows
    That hardly in a little thing
Love faileth of the work it does
    Till it grow ripe for gathering.

Six months, and now my sweet is dead
    A trouble takes me; I know not
If all were done well, all well said,
    No word or tender deed forgot.

Too sweet, for the least part in her,
    To have shed life out by fragments; yet,
Could the close mouth catch breath and stir,
    I might see something I forget.

Six months, and I sit still and hold
    In two cold palms her cold two feet.
Her hair, half grey half ruined gold,
    Thrills me and burns me in kissing it.

Love bites and stings me through, to see
    Her keen face made of sunken bones.
Her worn-off eyelids madden me,
    That were shot through with purple once.

She said, 'Be good with me; I grow
    So tired for shame's sake, I shall die
If you say nothing'; even so.
    And she is dead now, and shame put by.

Yea, and the scorn she had of me
    In the old time, doubtless vexed her then.
I never should have kissed her. See
    What fools God's anger makes of men!

She might have loved me a little too,
    Had I been humbler for her sake.
But that new shame could make love new
    She saw not—yet her shame did make.

I took too much upon my love,
    Having for such mean service done
Her beauty and all the ways thereof,
    Her face and all the sweet thereon.

Yea, all this while I tended her,
    I know the old love held fast his part:
I know the old scorn waxed heavier,
    Mixed with sad wonder, in her heart.

It may be all my love went wrong—
    A scribe's work writ awry and blurred,
Scrawled after the blind evensong—
    Spoilt music with no perfect word.

But surely I would fain have done
   All things the best I could. Perchance
Because I failed, came short of one,
   She kept at heart that other man's.

I am grown blind with all these things:
   It may be now she hath in sight
Some better knowledge: still there clings
   The old question. Will not God do right?

Lines from APRIL

From the French of the Vidame de Chartres

12 - -?

When the fields catch flower
   And the underwood is green,
And from bower unto bower
   The songs of the birds begin,
   I sing with sighing between.
When I laugh and sing,
   I am heavy at heart for my sin;
I am sad in the spring
   For my love that I shall not win,
For a foolish thing.

This profit I have of my woe,
   That I know, as I sing,
I know he will needs have it so
   Who is master and king,
   Who is lord of the spirit of spring.
I will serve her and will not spare
   Till her pity awake
Who is good, who is pure, who is fair,
   Even her for whose sake.
Love hath ta'en me and slain unaware.

MADONNA MIA

Under green apple-boughs
That never a storm will rouse,
My lady hath her house
   Between two bowers;
In either of the twain
Red roses full of rain;
She hath for bondwomen
   All kind of flowers.

She hath no handmaid fair
To draw her curled gold hair
Through rings of gold that bear
   Her whole hair's weight;
She hath no maids to stand
Gold-clothed on either hand;
In all the great green land
   None is so great.

She hath no more to wear
But one white hood of vair
Drawn over eyes and hair,
   Wrought with strange gold,
Made for some great queen's head,
Some fair great queen since dead;
And one strait gown of red
   Against the cold.

Beneath her eyelids deep
Love lying seems asleep,
Love, swift to wake, to weep,
   To laugh, to gaze;
Her breasts are like white birds,
And all her gracious words
As water-grass to herds
   In the June-days.

To her all dews that fall
And rains are musical;
Her flowers are fed from all,
   Her joy from these;
In the deep-feathered firs
Their gift of joy is hers,
In the least breath that stirs
   Across the trees.

She grows with greenest leaves,
Ripens with reddest sheaves,
Forgets, remembers, grieves,
   And is not sad;
The quiet lands and skies
Leave light upon her eyes;
None knows her, weak or wise,
   Or tired or glad.

None knows, none understands,
What flowers are like her hands;
Though you should search all lands
   Wherein time grows,

What snows are like her feet,
Though his eyes burn with heat
Through gazing on my sweet,
   Yet no man knows.

Only this thing is said;
That white and gold and red,
God's three chief words, man's bread
   And oil and wine,
Were given her for dowers,
And kingdom of all hours,
And grace of goodly flowers
   And various vine.

This is my lady's praise:
God after many days
Wrought her in unknown ways,
   In sunset lands;
This was my lady's birth;
God gave her might and mirth
And laid his whole sweet earth
   Between her hands.

Under deep apple-boughs
My lady hath her house;
She wears upon her brows
   The flower thereof;
All saying but what God saith
To her is as vain breath;
She is more strong than death,
   Being strong as love.

A BALLAD OF BURDENS

The burden of fair women. Vain delight,
  And love self-slain in some sweet shameful way,
And sorrowful old age that comes by night
  As a thief comes that has no heart by day,
  And change that finds fair cheeks and leaves them grey,
And weariness that keeps awake for hire,
  And grief that says what pleasure used to say,
This is the end of every man's desire.

The burden of bought kisses. This is sore,
  A burden without fruit in childbearing;
Between the nightfall and the dawn threescore,
  Threescore between the dawn and evening.
  The shuddering in thy lips, the shuddering
In thy sad eyelids tremulous like fire,
  Makes love seem shameful and a wretched thing.
This is the end of every man's desire.

The burden of sweet speeches. Nay, kneel down,
  Cover thy head, and weep; for verily
These market-men that buy thy white and brown
  In the last days shall take no thought for thee.
  In the last days like earth thy face shall be.
Yea, like sea-marsh made thick with brine and mire,
  Sad with sick leavings of the sterile sea.
This is the end of every man's desire.

The burden of long living. Thou shalt fear
  Waking, and sleeping mourn upon thy bed;
And say at night 'Would God the day were here,'
  And say at dawn 'Would God the day were dead.'
  With weary days thou shalt be clothed and fed,
And wear remorse of heart for thine attire,
  Pain for thy girdle and sorrow upon thine head;
This is the end of every man's desire.

The burden of bright colours. Thou shalt see
  Gold tarnished, and the grey above the green;
And as the thing thou seest thy face shall be,
  And no more as the thing beforetime seen.
  And thou shalt say of mercy 'It hath been',
And living, watch the old lips and loves expire,
  And talking, tears shall take thy breath between.
This is the end of every man's desire.

The burden of sad sayings. In that day
  Thou shalt tell all thy days and hours, and tell
Thy times and ways and words of love, and say
  How one was dear and one desirable,
  And sweet was life to hear and sweet to smell,
But now with lights reverse the old hours retire
  And the last hour is shod with fire from hell.
This is the end of every man's desire.

The burden of four seasons. Rain in spring,
  White rain and wind among the tender trees:
A summer of green sorrows gathering,
  Rank autumn in a mist of miseries,

With sad face set towards the year, that sees
The charred ash drop out of the dropping pyre,
   And winter wan with many maladies;
This is the end of every man's desire.

The burden of dead faces. Out of sight
   And out of love, beyond the reach of hands,
Changed in the changing of the dark and light,
   They walk and weep about the barren lands
   Where no seed is nor any garner stands,
Where in short breaths the doubtful days respire,
   And time's turned glass lets through the sighing sands;
This is the end of every man's desire.

The burden of much gladness. Life and lust
   Forsake thee, and the face of thy delight;
And underfoot the heavy hour strews dust,
   And overhead strange weathers burn and bite;
   And where the red was, lo the bloodless white,
And where truth was, the likeness of a liar,
   And where day was, the likeness of the night;
This is the end of every man's desire.

L'ENVOY

Princes, and ye whom pleasure quickeneth,
   Heed well this rhyme before your pleasure tire;
For life is sweet, but after life is death.
   This is the end of every man's desire.

ILICET

There is an end of joy and sorrow;
Peace all day long, all night, all morrow,
   But never a time to laugh or weep.
The end is come of pleasant places,
The end of tender words and faces,
   The end of all, the poppied sleep.

No place for sound within their hearing,
No room to hope, no time for fearing,
   No lips to laugh, no lids for tears.
The old years have run out all their measure;
No chance of pain, no chance of pleasure,
   No fragment of the broken years.

Outside of all the worlds and ages,
There where the fool is as the sage is,
   There where the slayer is clean of blood,
No end, no passage, no beginning,
There where the sinner leaves off sinning,
   There where the good man is not good.

There is not one thing with another,
But Evil saith to Good: My brother,
   My brother, I am one with thee:
They shall not strive nor cry for ever:
No man shall choose between them: never
   Shall this thing end and that thing be.

Wind wherein seas and stars are shaken
Shall shake them, and they shall not waken;
  None that has lain down shall arise;
The stones are sealed across their places;
One shadow is shed on all their faces,
  One blindness cast on all their eyes.

Sleep, is it sleep perchance that covers
Each face, as each face were his lover's?
  Farewell; as men that sleep fare well.
The grave's mouth laughs unto derision
Desire and dread and dream and vision,
  Delight of heaven and sorrow of hell.

No soul shall tell nor lip shall number
The names and tribes of you that slumber;
  No memory, no memorial.
  'Thou knowest'—who shall say thou knowest?
There is none highest and none lowest:
  An end, an end, an end of all.

Good night, good sleep, good rest from sorrow,
To these that shall not have good morrow;
  The gods be gentle to all these.
Nay, if death be not, how shall they be?
Nay, is there help in heaven? it may be
  All things and lords of things shall cease.

The stooped urn, filling, dips and flashes;
The bronzèd brims are deep in ashes;
  The pale old lips of death are fed.
Shall this dust gather flesh hereafter?
Shall one shed tears or fall to laughter,
  At sight of all these poor old dead?

Nay, as thou wilt; these know not of it;
Thine eyes' strong weeping shall not profit,
   Thy laughter shall not give thee ease;
Cry aloud, spare not, cease not crying,
Sigh, till thou cleave thy sides with sighing,
   Thou shalt not raise up one of these.

Burnt spices flash, and burnt wine hisses,
The breathing flame's mouth curls and kisses
   The small dried rows of frankincense;
All round the sad red blossoms smoulder,
Flowers coloured like the fire, but colder,
   In sign of sweet things taken hence;

Yea, for their sake and in death's favour
Things of sweet shape and of sweet savour
   We yield them, spice and flower and wine;
Yea, costlier things than wine or spices,
Whereof none knoweth how great the price is,
   And fruit that comes not of the vine.

From boy's pierced throat and girl's pierced bosom
   Drips, reddening round the blood-red blossom,
     The slow delicious bright soft blood,
Bathing the spices and the pyre,
Bathing the flowers and fallen fire,
   Bathing the blossom by the bud.

Roses whose lips the flame has deadened
Drink till the lapping leaves are reddened
   And warm wet inner petals weep;
The flower whereof sick sleep gets leisure,
Barren of balm and purple pleasure,
   Fumes with no native steam of sleep.

Why will ye weep? what do ye weeping?
For waking folk and people sleeping,
   And sands that fill and sands that fall,
The days rose-red, the poppied hours,
Blood, wine, and spice and fire and flowers,
   There is one end of one and all.

Shall such an one lend love or borrow?
Shall these be sorry for thy sorrow?
   Shall these give thanks for words or breath?
Their hate is as their loving-kindness;
The frontlet of their brows is blindness,
   The armlet of their arms is death.

Lo, for no noise or light of thunder
Shall these grave-clothes be rent in sunder,
   He that hath taken, shall he give?
He hath rent them: shall he bind together?
He hath bound them, shall he break the tether?
He hath slain them: shall he bid them live?

A little sorrow, a little pleasure,
Fate metes us from the dusty measure
   That holds the date of all of us;
We are born with travail and strong crying,
And from the birth-day to the dying
   The likeness of our life is thus.

One girds himself to serve another,
Whose father was the dust, whose mother
   The little dead red worm therein;
They find no fruit of things they cherish;
The goodness of a man shall perish,
   It shall be one thing with his sin.

In deep wet ways by grey old gardens
Fed with sharp spring the sweet fruit hardens;
   They know not what fruits wane or grow;
Red summer burns to the utmost ember;
They know not, neither can remember,
   The old years and flowers they used to know.

Ah, for their sakes, so trapped and taken,
For theirs, forgotten and forsaken,
   Watch, sleep not, gird thyself with prayer.
Nay, where the heart of wrath is broken,
Where long love ends as a thing spoken,
   How shall thy crying enter there?

Though the iron sides of the old world falter
The likeness of them shall not alter
   For all the rumour of periods,
The stars and seasons that come after,
The tears of latter men, the laughter
   Of the old unalterable gods.

Far up above the years and nations,
The high gods, clothed and crowned with patience,
   Endure through days of death-like date;
They bear the witness of things hidden;
Before their eyes all life stands chidden,
   As they before the eyes of Fate.

Not for their love shall Fate retire,
Nor they relent for our desire,
   Nor the graves open for their call.
The end is more than joy and anguish,
Than lives that laugh and lives that languish,
   The poppied sleep, the end of all.

Lines from ANACTORIA

For who shall change with prayers or thanksgivings
The mystery of the cruelty of things?
Or say what God above all gods and years,
With offering and blood-sacrifice of tears,
With lamentation from strange lands, from graves
Where the snake pastures, from scarred mouths of slaves,
From prison, and from plunging prows of ships
Through flamelike foam of the sea's closing lips—
With thwartings of strange signs, and wind-blown hair
Of comets, desolating the dim air,
When darkness is made fast with seals and bars,
And fierce reluctance of disastrous stars,
Eclipse, and sound of shaken hills, and wings
Darkening, and blind inexpiable things—
With sorrow of labouring moons, and altering light
And travail of the planets of the night,
And weeping of the weary Pleiads seven,
Feeds the mute melancholy lust of heaven?
Is not this incense bitterness, his meat
Murder? his hidden face and iron feet
Hath not man known, and felt them on their way
Threaten and trample all things and every day?
Hath he not sent us hunger? who hath cursed
Spirit and flesh with longing? filled with thirst
Their lips who cried unto him? who bade exceed
The fervid will, fall short the feeble deed,

Bade sink the spirit and the flesh aspire,
Pain animate the dust of dead desire,
And life yield up her flower to violent fate?
Him would I reach, him smite, him desecrate,
Pierce the cold lips of God with human breath,
And mix his immortality with death.
Why hath he made us? what had all we done
That we should live and loathe the sterile sun,
And with the moon wax paler as she wanes,
And pulse by pulse feel time grow through our veins?
Thee too the years shall cover; thou shalt be
As the rose born of one same blood with thee,
As a song sung, as a word said, and fall
Flower-wise, and be not any more at all,
Nor any memory of thee anywhere;
For never Muse has bound above thine hair
The high Pierian flower whose graft outgrows
All summer kinship of the mortal rose
And colour of deciduous days, nor shed
Reflex and flush of heaven about thine head,
Nor reddened brows made pale by floral grief
With splendid shadow from that lordlier leaf.
Yea, thou shalt be forgotten like spilt wine,
Except these kisses of my lips on thine
Brand them with immortality; but me—
Men shall not see bright fire nor hear the sea,
Nor mix their hearts with music, nor behold
Cast forth of heaven with feet of awful gold
And plumeless wings that make the bright air blind,
Lightning, with thunder for a hound behind
Hunting through fields unfurrowed and unsown—
But in the light and laughter, in the moan
And music, and in grasp of lip and hand

And shudder of water that makes felt on land
The immeasurable tremor of all the sea,
Memories shall mix and metaphors of me.
Like me shall be the shuddering calm of night,
When all the winds of the world for pure delight
Close lips that quiver and fold up wings that ache;
When nightingales are louder for love's sake,
And leaves tremble like lute-strings or like fire;
Like me the one star swooning with desire
Even at the cold lips of the sleepless moon,
As I at thine; like me the waste white noon,
Burnt through with barren sunlight; and like me
The land-stream and the tide-stream in the sea.
I am sick with time as these with ebb and flow,
And by the yearning in my veins I know
The yearning sound of waters; and mine eyes
Burn as that beamless fire which fills the skies
With troubled stars and travailing things of flame;
And in my heart the grief consuming them
Labours, and in my veins the thirst of these,
And all the summer travail of the trees
And all the winter sickness; and the earth,
Filled full with deadly works of death and birth,
Some spent with hungry lusts of birth and death,
Has pain like mine in her divided breath;
Her spring of leaves is barren, and her fruit
Ashes; her boughs are burdened, and her root
Fibrous and gnarled with poison; underneath
Serpents have gnawn it through with tortuous teeth
Made sharp upon the bones of all the dead,
And wild birds rend her branches overhead.
These, woven as raiment for his word and thought,
These hath God made, and me as these, and wrought

Song, and hath lit it at my lips; and me
Earth shall not gather though she feed on thee.
As a shed tear shalt thou be shed; but I—
Lo, earth may labour, men live long and die,
Years change and stars, and the high God devise
New things, and old things wane before his eyes
Who wields and wrecks them, being more strong than
                                       they—
But, having made me, me he shall not slay.
Nor slay nor satiate, like those herds of his
Who laugh and live a little, and their kiss
Contents them, and their loves are swift and sweet,
And sure death grasps and gains them with slow feet,
Love they or hate they, strive or bow their knees—
And all these end; he hath his will of these.
Yea, but albeit he slay me, hating me—
Albeit he hide me in the deep dear sea
And cover me with cool wan foam, and ease
This soul of mine as any soul of these,
And give me water and great sweet waves, and make
The very sea's name lordlier for my sake,
The whole sea sweeter—albeit I die indeed
And hide myself and sleep and no man heed,
Of me the high God hath not all his will.
Blossom of branches, and on each high hill
Clear air and wind, and under in clamorous vales
Fierce noises of the fiery nightingales,
Buds burning in the sudden spring like fire,
The wan washed sand and the waves' vain desire,
Sails seen like blown white flowers at sea, and words
That bring tears swiftest, and long notes of birds
Violently singing till the whole world sings—
I, Sappho, shall be one with all these things,

With all high things for ever; and my face
Seen once, my songs once heard in a strange place,
Cleave to men's lives, and waste the days thereof
With gladness and much sadness and long love.
Yea, they shall say, earth's womb has borne in vain
New things, and never this best thing again;
Borne days and men, borne fruits and wars and wine,
Seasons and songs, but no song more like mine.
And they shall know me as ye who have known me here,
Last year when I loved Atthis, and this year
When I love thee, and they shall praise me, and say
'She hath all time as all we have our day,
Shall she not live and have her will'—even I?
Yea, though thou diest, I say I shall not die.
For these shall give me of their souls, shall give
Life, and the days and loves wherewith I live,
Shall quicken me with loving, fill with breath,
Save me and serve me, strive for me with death.
Alas, that neither moon nor snow nor dew
Nor all cold things can purge me wholly through,
Assuage me nor allay me nor appease,
Till supreme sleep shall being me bloodless ease;
Till time wax faint in all his periods;
Till fate undo the bondage of the gods,
And lay, to slake and satiate me all through,
Lotus and Lethe on my lips like dew,
And shed around and over and under me
Thick darkness and the insuperable sea.

SAPPHICS

All the night sleep came not upon my eyelids,
Shed not dew, nor shook nor unclosed a feather,
Yet with lips shut close and with eyes of iron
    Stood and beheld me.

Then to me so lying awake a vision
Came without sleep over the seas and touched me,
Softly touched mine eyelids and lips; and I too,
    Full of the vision,

Saw the white implacable Aphrodite,
Saw the hair unbound and the feet unsandalled
Shine as fire of sunset on western waters;
    Saw the reluctant

Feet, the straining plumes of the doves that drew her,
Looking always, looking with necks reverted,
Back to Lesbos, back to the hills whereunder
    Shone Mitylene;

Heard the flying feet of the Loves behind her
Make a sudden thunder upon the waters,
As the thunder flung from the strong unclosing
    Wings of a great wind.

So the goddess fled from her place, with awful
Sound of feet and thunder of wings around her;
While behind a clamour of singing women
   Severed the twilight.

Ah the singing, ah the delight, the passion!
All the Loves wept, listening; sick with anguish,
Stood the crowned nine Muses about Apollo;
   Fear was upon them,

While the tenth sang wonderful things they knew not.
Ah the tenth, the Lesbian! the nine were silent,
None endured the sound of her song for weeping:
   Laurel by laurel,

Faded all their crowns; but about her forehead,
Round her woven tresses and ashen temples
White as dead snow, paler than grass in summer,
   Ravaged with kisses,

Shone a light of fire as a crown for ever.
Yea, almost the implacable Aphrodite
Paused, and almost wept; such a song was that song,
   Yea, by her name too

Called her, saying, 'Turn to me, O my Sappho';
Yet she turned her face from the Loves, she saw not
Tears for laughter darken immortal eyelids,
   Heard not about her

Fearful fitful wings of the doves departing,
Saw not how the bosom of Aphrodite
Shook with weeping, saw not her shaken raiment,
   Saw not her hands wrung;

Saw the Lesbians kissing across their smitten
Lutes with lips more sweet than the sound of lute-strings,
Mouth to mouth and hand upon hand, her chosen,
   Fairer than all men;

Only saw the beautiful lips and fingers,
Full of songs and kisses and little whispers,
Full of music; only beheld among them
   Soar, as a bird soars

Newly fledged, her visible song, a marvel,
Made of perfect sound and exceeding passion,
Sweetly shapen, terrible, full of thunders,
   Clothed with the wind's wings.

Then rejoiced she, laughing with love, and scattered
Roses, awful roses of holy blossom;
Then the Loves thronged sadly with hidden faces
   Round Aphrodite,

Then the Muses, stricken at heart, were silent,
Yea, the gods waxed pale; such a song was that song.
All reluctant, all with a fresh repulsion,
   Fled from before her.

All withdrew long since, and the land was barren,
Full of fruitless women and music only.
Now perchance, when winds are assuaged at sunset,
   Lulled at the dewfall,

By the grey sea-side, unassuaged, unheard of,
Unbeloved, unseen in the ebb of twilight,
Ghosts of outcast women return lamenting,
   Purged not in Lethe,

Clothed about with flame and with tears, and singing
Songs that move the heart of the shaken heaven,
Songs that break the heart of the earth with pity,
  Hearing, to hear them.

HENDECASYLLABICS

In the month of the long decline of roses
I, beholding the summer dead before me,
Set my face to the sea and journeyed silent,
Gazing eagerly where above the sea-mark
Flame as fierce as the fervid eyes of lions
Half divided the eyelids of the sunset;
Till I heard as it were a noise of waters
Moving tremulous under feet of angels
Multitudinous, out of all the heavens;
Knew the fluttering wind, the fluttered foliage,
Shaken fitfully, full of sound and shadow;
And saw, trodden upon by noiseless angels,
Long mysterious reaches fed with moonlight,
Sweet sad straits in a soft subsiding channel,
Blown about by the lips of winds I knew not,
Winds not born in the north nor any quarter,
Winds not warm with the south nor any sunshine;
Heard between them a voice of exultation,
'Lo, the summer is dead, the sun is faded,
Even like as a leaf the year is withered,
All the fruits of the day from all her branches
Gathered, neither is any left to gather.
All the flowers are dead, the tender blossoms,
All are taken away; the season wasted,
Like an ember among the fallen ashes.
Now with light of the winter days, with moonlight,

Light of snow, and the bitter light of hoarfrost,
We bring flowers that fade not after autumn,
Pale white chaplets and crowns of latter seasons,
Fair false leaves (but the summer leaves were falser),
Woven under the eyes of stars and planets
When low light was upon the windy reaches
Where the flower of foam was blown, a lily
Dropt among the sonorous fruitless furrows
And green fields of the sea that make no pasture:
Since the winter begins, the weeping winter,
All whose flowers are tears, and round his temples
Iron blossom of frost is bound for ever.'

BEFORE PARTING

A month or twain to live on honeycomb
Is pleasant; but one tires of scented time,
Cold sweet recurrence of accepted rhyme,
And that strong purple under juice and foam
Where the wine's heart has burst;
Nor feel the latter kisses like the first.

Once yet, this poor one time; I will not pray
Even to change the bitterness of it,
The bitter taste ensuing on the sweet,
To make your tears fall where your soft hair lay
All blurred and heavy in some perfumed wise
Over my face and eyes.

And yet who knows what end the scythèd wheat
Makes of its foolish poppies' mouths of red?
These were not sown, these are not harvested,
They grow a month and are cast under feet
And none has care thereof,
As none has care of a divided love.

I know each shadow of your lips by rote,
Each change of love in eyelids and eyebrows;
The fashion of fair temples tremulous
With tender blood, and colour of your throat;
I know not how love is gone out of this,
Seeing that all was his.

Love's likeness there endures upon all these:
But out of these one shall not gather love.
Day hath not strength nor the night shade enough
To make love whole and fill his lips with ease,
As some bee-builded cell
Feels at filled lips the heavy honey swell.

I know not how this last month leaves your hair
Less full of purple colour and hid spice,
And that luxurious trouble of closed eyes
Is mixed with meaner shadow and waste care;
And love, kissed out by pleasure, seems not yet
Worth patience to regret.

THE SUNDEW

A little marsh-plant, yellow green,
And pricked at lip with tender red.
Tread close, and either way you tread
Some faint black water jets between
Lest you should bruise the curious head.

A live thing maybe; who shall know?
The summer knows and suffers it;
For the cool moss is thick and sweet
Each side, and saves the blossom so
That it lives out the long June heat.

The deep scent of the heather burns
About it; breathless though it be,
Bow down and worship; more than we
Is the least flower whose life returns,
Least weed renascent in the sea.

We are vexed and cumbered in earth's sight
With wants, with many memories;
These see their mother what she is,
Glad-growing, till August leave more bright
The apple-coloured cranberries.

Wind blows and bleaches the strong grass,
Blown all one way to shelter it

From trample of strayed kine, with feet
Felt heavier than the moorhen was,
Strayed up past patches of wild wheat.

You call it sundew: how it grows,
If with its colour it have breath,
If life taste sweet to it, if death
Pain its soft petal, no man knows:
Man has no sight or sense that saith.

My sundew, grown of gentle days,
In these green miles the spring begun
Thy growth ere April had half done
With the soft secret of her ways
Or June made ready for the sun.

O red-lipped mouth of marsh-flower,
I have a secret halved with thee.
The name that is love's name to me
Thou knowest, and the face of her
Who is my festival to see.

The hard sun, as thy petals knew,
Coloured the heavy moss-water:
Thou wert not worth green midsummer
Nor fit to live to August blue,
O sundew, not remembering her.

AUGUST

There were four apples on the bough,
Half gold half red, that one might know
The blood was ripe inside the core;
The colour of the leaves was more
Like stems of yellow corn that grow
Through all the gold June meadow's floor.

The warm smell of the fruit was good
To feed on, and the spilt green wood,
With all its bearded lips and stains
Of mosses in the cloven veins,
Most pleasant, if one lay or stood
In sunshine or in happy rains.

There were four apples on the tree,
Red stained through gold, that all might see
The sun went warm from core to rind;
The green leaves made the summer blind
In that soft place they kept for me
With golden apples shut behind.

The leaves caught gold across the sun,
And where the bluest air begun,
Thirsted for song to help the heat;
As I to feel my lady's feet
Draw close before the day were done;
Both lips grew dry with dreams of it.

AUGUST

In the mute August afternoon
They trembled to some undertune
Of music in the silver air;
Great pleasure was it to be there
Till green turned duskier and the moon
Coloured the corn-sheaves like gold hair.

That August time it was delight
To watch the red moons wane to white
'Twixt grey seamed stems of apple-trees;
A sense of heavy harmonies
Grew on the growth of patient night,
More sweet than shapen music is.

But some three hours before the moon
The air, still eager from the noon,
Flagged after heat, not wholly dead;
Against the stem I leant my head;
The colour soothed me like a tune,
Green leaves all round the gold and red.

I lay there till the warm smell grew
More sharp, when flecks of yellow dew
Between the round ripe leaves had blurred
The rind with stain and wet; I heard
A wind that blew and breathed and blew,
Too weak to alter its one word.

The wet leaves next the gentle fruit
Felt smoother, and the brown tree-root
Felt the mould warmer: I too felt
(As water feels the slow gold melt
Right through it when the day burns mute)
The peace of time wherein love dwelt.

There were four apples on the tree,
Gold stained on red that all might see
The sweet blood filled them to the core:
The colour of her hair is more
Like stems of fair faint gold, that be
Mown from the harvest's middle-floor.

THE KING'S DAUGHTER

We were ten maidens in the green corn,
    Small red leaves in the mill-water:
Fairer maidens never were born,
    Apples of gold for the king's daughter.

We were ten maidens by a well-head,
    Small white birds in the mill-water:
Sweeter maidens never were wed,
    Rings of red for the king's daughter.

The first to spin, the second to sing,
    Seeds of wheat in the mill-water;
The third may was a goodly thing,
    White bread and brown for the king's daughter.

The fourth to sew and the fifth to play,
    Fair green weed in the mill-water;
The sixth may was a goodly may,
    White wine and red for the king's daughter.

The seventh to woo, the eighth to wed,
    Fair thin reeds in the mill-water;
The ninth had gold work on her head,
    Honey in the comb for the king's daughter.

The ninth had gold work round her hair,
   Fallen flowers in the mill-water;
The tenth may was goodly and fair,
   Golden gloves for the king's daughter.

We were ten maidens in a field green,
   Fallen fruit in the mill-water;
Fairer maidens never have been
   Golden sleeves for the king's daughter.

By there comes the king's young son,
   A little wind in the mill-water;
'Out of ten maidens ye'll grant me one',
   A crown of red for the king's daughter.

'Out of ten mays ye'll give me the best',
   A little rain in the mill-water;
A bed of yellow straw for all the rest,
   A bed of gold for the king's daughter.

He's ta'en out the goodliest,
   Rain that rains in the mill-water;
A comb of yellow shell for all the rest,
   A comb of gold for the king's daughter.

He's made her bed to the goodliest,
   Wind and hail in the mill-water;
A grass girdle for all the rest,
   A girdle of arms for the king's daughter.

He's set his heart to the goodliest,
   Snow that snows in the mill-water;
Nine little kisses for all the rest,
   An hundredfold for the king's daughter.

He's ta'en his leave at the goodliest,
  Broken boats in the mill-water;
Golden gifts for all the rest,
  Sorrow of heart for the king's daughter.

'Ye'll make a grave for my fair body',
  Running rain in the mill-water;
'And ye'll streek my brother at the side of me',
  The pains of hell for the king's daughter.

AFTER DEATH

The four boards of the coffin lid
Heard all the dead man did.

The first curse was in his mouth,
Made of grave's mould and deadly drouth.

The next curse was in his head,
Made of God's work discomfited.

The next curse was in his hands,
Made out of two grave-bands.

The next curse was in his feet,
Made out of a grave-sheet.

'I had fair coins red and white,
And my name was as great light;

I had fair clothes green and red,
And strong gold bound round my head.

But no meat comes in my mouth,
Now I fare as the worm doth;

And no gold binds in my hair,
Now I fare as the blind fare.

My live thews were of great strength,
Now am I waxen a span's length,

My live sides were full of lust,
Now are they dried with dust.'

The first board spake and said:
'Is it best eating flesh or bread?'

The second answered it:
'Is wine or honey the more sweet?'

The third board spake and said:
'Is red gold worth a girl's gold head?'

The fourth made answer thus:
'All these things are as one with us.'

The dead man asked of them:
'Is the green land stained brown with flame?

Have they hewn my son for beasts to eat,
And my wife's body for beasts' meat?

Have they boiled my maid in a brass pan,
And built a gallows to hang my man?'

The boards said to him:
'This is a lewd thing that ye deem.

Your wife has gotten a golden bed,
All the sheets are sewn with red.

Your son has gotten a coat of silk,
The sleeves are soft as curded milk.

Your maid has gotten a kirtle new,
All the skirt has braids of blue.

Your man has gotten both ring and glove,
Wrought well for eyes to love.'

The dead man answered thus:
'What good gift shall God give us?'

The boards answered him anon:
'Flesh to feed hell's worm upon.'

THE SEA-SWALLOWS

This fell when Christmas lights were done,
 Red rose leaves will never make wine;
But before the Easter lights begun;
 The ways are sair fra' the Till to the Tyne.

Two lovers sat where the rowan blows
 And all the grass is heavy and fine,
By the gathering place of the sea-swallows
 When the wind brings them over Tyne.

Blossom of broom will never make bread,
 Red rose leaves will never make wine;
Between her brows she is grown red
 That was full white in the fields by Tyne.

'O what is this thing ye have on,
 Show me now, sweet daughter of mine?'
'O father, this is my little son
 That I found hid in the sides of Tyne.

'O what will ye give my son to eat,
 Red rose leaves will never make wine?'
'Fen-water and adder's meat,
 The ways are sair fra' the Till to the Tyne.'

'Or what will ye get my son to wear,
    Red rose leaves will never make wine?'
'A weed and a web of nettle's hair,
    The ways are sair fra' the Till to the Tyne.'

'Or what will ye take to line his bed,
    Red rose leaves will never make wine?'
'Two black stones at the kirkwall's head,
    The ways are sair fra' the Till to the Tyne.'

'Or what will ye give my son for land,
    Red rose leaves will never make wine?'
'Three girl's paces of red sand,
    The ways are sair fra' the Till to the Tyne.'

'Or what will ye give me for my son,
    Red rose leaves will never make wine?'
'Six times to kiss his young mouth on,
    The ways are sair fra' the Till to the Tyne.'

'But what have ye done with the bearing-bread,
    And what have ye made of the washing-wine?
Or where have ye made your bearing-bed,
    To bear a son in the sides of Tyne?'

'The bearing-bread is soft and new,
    There is no soil in the straining wine;
The bed was made between green and blue,
    It stands full soft by the sides of Tyne.

'The fair grass was my bearing-bread,
    The well-water my washing-wine;
The low leaves were my bearing-bed,
    And that was best in the sides of Tyne.'

'O daughter, if ye have done this thing,
   I wot the greater grief is mine;
This was a bitter child-bearing,
   When ye were got by the sides of Tyne.

'About the time of sea-swallows
   That fly full thick by six and nine,
Ye'll have my body out of the house,
   To bury me by the sides of Tyne.

'Set nine stones by the wall for twain,
   Red rose leaves will never make wine;
For the bed I take will measure ten,
   The ways are sair fra' the Till to the Tyne.

'Tread twelve girl's paces out for three,
   Red rose leaves will never make wine;
For the pit I made has taken me,
   The ways are sair fra' the Till to the Tyne.'

A CHRISTMAS CAROL

Three damsels in the queen's chamber,
   The queen's mouth was most fair;
She spake a word of God's mother
   As the combs went in her hair.
      Mary that is of might,
      Bring us to thy Son's sight.

They held the gold combs out from her,
   A span's length off her head;
She sang this song of God's mother
   And of her bearing-bed.
      Mary most full of grace,
      Bring us to thy Son's face.

When she sat at Joseph's hand,
   She looked against her side;
And either way from the short silk band
   Her girdle was all wried.
      Mary that all good may,
      Bring us to thy Son's way.

Mary had three women for her bed,
   The twain were maidens clean;
The first of them had white and red,
   The third had riven green.
      Mary that is so sweet,
      Bring us to thy Son's feet.

She had three women for her hair,
  Two were gloved soft and shod;
The third had feet and fingers bare,
  She was the likest God.
     Mary that wieldeth land,
     Bring us to thy Son's hand.

She had three women for her ease,
  The twain were good women:
The first two were the two Maries,
  The third was Magdalen.
     Mary that perfect is,
     Bring us to thy Son's kiss.

Joseph had three workmen in his stall,
  To serve him well upon;
The first of them were Peter and Paul,
  The third of them was John.
     Mary, God's handmaiden,
     Bring us to thy Son's ken.

'If your child be none other man's,
  But if it be very mine,
The bedstead shall be gold two spans,
  The bedfoot silver fine.'
     Mary that made God mirth,
     Bring us to thy Son's birth.

'If the child be some other man's,
  And if it be none of mine,
The manger shall be straw two spans,
  Betwixen kine and kine.'
     Mary that made sin cease,
     Bring us to thy Son's peace.

Christ was born upon this wise,
   It fell on such a night,
Neither with sounds of psalteries,
   Nor with fire for light.
      Mary that is God's spouse,
      Bring us to thy Son's house.

The star came out upon the east
   With a great sound and sweet:
Kings gave gold to make him feast
   And myrrh for him to eat.
      Mary, of thy sweet mood,
      Bring us to thy Son's good.

He had two handmaids at his head,
   One handmaid at his feet;
The twain of them were fair and red
   The third one was right sweet.
      Mary that is most wise,
      Bring us to thy Son's eyes.   *Amen.*

THE MASQUE OF
QUEEN BERSABE

A Miracle-play

KING DAVID

Knights mine, all that be in hall,
I have a counsel to you all,
Because of this thing God lets fall
   Among us for a sign.
For some days hence as I did eat
From kingly dishes my good meat,
There flew a bird between my feet
   As red as any wine.
This bird had a long bill of red
And a gold ring above his head;
Long time he sat and nothing said,
Put softly down his neck and fed
   From the gilt patens fine:
And as I marvelled at the last
He shut his two keen eyën fast
And suddenly woxe big and brast
   Ere one should tell to nine.

PRIMUS MILES

Sir, note this that I will say;
That Lord who maketh corn with hay
And morrows each of yesterday,
   He hath you in his hand.

SECUNDUS MILES (*Paganus quidam*)

By Satan I hold no such thing;
For if wine swell within a king
Whose ears for drink are hot and ring,
The same shall dream of wine-bibbing
    Whilst he can lie or stand.

QUEEN BERSABE

Peace now, lords, for Godis head.
Ye chirk as starlings that be fed
And gape as fishes newly dead;
The devil put your bones to bed,
    Lo, this is all to say.

SECUNDUS MILES

By Mahound, lords, I have good will
This devil's bird to wring and spill;
For now meseems our game goes ill,
    Ye have scant hearts to play.

TERTIUS MILES

Lo, sirs, this word is there said,
That Urias the knight is dead
Through some ill craft; by Poulis head,
I doubt his blood hath made so red
This bird that flew from the queen's bed
    Whereof ye have such fear.

KING DAVID

Yea, my good knave, and is it said
That I can raise men from the dead?
By God I think to have his head

Who saith words of my lady's bed
   For any thief to hear.
     Et percutiat eum in capite.

QUEEN BERSABE

I wis men shall spit at me,
And say it were but right for thee
That one should hang thee on a tree;
Ho! it were a fair thing to see
The big stones bruise her false body;
   Fie! who shall see her dead?

KING DAVID

I rede you have no fear of this,
For as ye wot, the first good kiss
I had must be the last of his;
Now are ye queen of mine, I wis,
And lady of a house that is
   Full rich of meat and bread.

PRIMUS MILES

I bid you make good cheer to be
So fair a queen as all men see.
And hold us for your lieges free;
By Peter's soul that hath the key,
   Ye have good hap of it.

SECUNDUS MILES

I would that he were hanged and dead
Who hath no joy to see your head
With gold about it, barred on red;
I hold him as a sow of lead
   That is so scant of wit

Tunc dicat NATHAN *propheta.*

O king, I have a word to thee;
The child that is in Bersabe
Shall wither without light to see;
This word is come of God by me
    For sin that ye have done.
Because herein ye did not right,
To take the fair one lamb to smite
That was of Urias the knight;
    Ye wist he had but one.
Full many sheep I wot ye had,
And many women, when ye bade
To do your will and keep you glad;
And a good crown about your head
    With gold to show thereon.
This Urias had one poor house
With low-barred latoun shot-windows
And scant of corn to fill a mouse;
And rusty basnets for his brows,
    To wear them to the bone.
Yea the roofs also, as men sain,
Were thin to hold against the rain;
Therefore what rushes were there lain
Grew wet withouten foot of men;
The stancheons were all gone in twain
    As sick man's flesh is gone.
Nathless he had great joy to see
The long hair of this Bersabe
Fall round her lap and round her knee
Even to her small soft feet, that be
Shod now with crimson royally
    And covered with clean gold.

Likewise great joy he had to kiss
Her throat, where now the scarlet is
Against her little chin, I wis,
    That then was but cold.
No scarlet then her kirtle had
And little gold about it sprad;
But her red mouth was always glad
To kiss, albeit the eyes were sad
    With love they had to hold.

SECUNDUS MILES

How! old thief, thy wits are lame;
To clip such it is no shame:
I rede you in the devil's name,
Ye come not here to make men game;
By Termagaunt that maketh grame,
    I shall to-bete thine head.
    Hic Diabolus capiat eum.
This knave hath sharp fingers, perfay;
Mahound you thank and keep alway,
And give you good knees to pray;
What man hath no lust to play,
The devil wring his ears, I say;
There is no more but wellaway,
    For now am I dead.

KING DAVID

Certes his mouth is wried and black,
Full little pence be in his sack;
This devil hath him by the back,
    It is no boot to lie.

NATHAN

Sitteth now still and learn of me
A little while and ye shall see
The face of God's strength presently.
All queens made as this Bersabe,
All that were fair and foul ye be,
    Come hither; it am I.
    Et hìc omnes cantabunt.

HERODIAS

I am the queen Herodias.
This headband of my temples was
    King Herod's gold band woven me,
This broken dry staff in my hand
Was the queen's staff of a great land
    Betwixen Perse and Samarie.
For that one dancing of my feet,
The fire is come in my green wheat,
    From one sea to the other sea.

AHOLIBAH

I am the queen Aholibah.
My lips kissed dumb the word of *Ah*
    Sighed on strange lips grown sick thereby
God wrought to me my royal bed;
The inner work thereof was red,
    The outer work was ivory.
My mouth's heat was the heat of flame
For lust towards the kings that came
    With horsemen riding royally.

CLEOPATRA

I am the queen of Ethiope.
Love bade my kissing eyelids ope
    That men beholding might praise love.
My hair was wonderful and curled;
My lips held fast the mouth o' the world
    To spoil the strength and speech thereof.
The latter triumph in my breath
Bowed down the beaten brows of death,
    Ashamed they had not wrath enough.

ABIHAIL

I am the queen of Tyrians.
My hair was glorious for twelve spans,
    That dried to loose dust afterward.
My stature was a strong man's length:
My neck was like a place of strength
    Built with white walls, even and hard.
Like the first noise of rain leaves catch
One from another, snatch by snatch,
    Is my praise, hissed against and marred.

AZUBAH

I am the queen of Amorites.
My face was like a place of lights
    With multitudes at festival.
The glory of my gracious brows
Was like God's house made glorious
    With colours upon either wall.
Between my brows and hair there was
A white space like a space of glass
    With golden candles over all.

AHOLAH

I am the queen of Amalek.
There was no tender touch or fleck
   To spoil my body or bared feet.
My words were soft like dulcimers,
And the first sweet of grape-flowers
   Made each side of my bosom sweet.
My raiment was as tender fruit
Whose rind smells sweet of spice-tree root,
   Bruised balm-blossom and budded wheat.

AHINOAM

I am the queen Ahinoam.
Like the throat of a soft slain lamb
   Was my throat, softer veined than his:
My lips were as two grapes the sun
Lays his whole weight of heat upon
   Like a mouth heavy with a kiss:
My hair's pure purple a wrought fleece,
My temples therein as a piece
   Of a pomegranate's cleaving is.

ATARAH

I am the queen Sidonian.
My face made faint the face of man,
   And strength was bound between my brows.
Spikenard was hidden in my ships,
Honey and wheat and myrrh in strips,
   White wools that shine as colour does,
Soft linen dyed upon the fold,
Split spice and cores of scented gold,
   Cedar and broken calamus.

SEMIRAMIS

I am the queen Semiramis.
The whole world and the sea that is
  In fashion like a chrysopras,
The noise of all men labouring,
The priest's mouth tired through thanksgiving,
  The sound of love in the blood's pause,
The strength of love in the blood's beat,
All these were cast beneath my feet
  And all found lesser than I was.

HESIONE

I am the queen Hesione.
The seasons that increased in me
  Made my face fairer than all men's.
I had the summer in my hair;
And all the pale gold autumn air
  Was as the habit of my sense.
My body was as fire that shone;
God's beauty that makes all things one
  Was one among my handmaidens.

CHRYSOTHEMIS

I am the queen of Samothrace.
God, making roses, made my face
  As a rose filled up full with red.
My prows made sharp the straitened seas
From Pontus to that Chersonese
  Whereon the ebbed Asian stream is shed.
My hair was as sweet scent that drips;
Love's breath begun about my lips
  Kindled the lips of people dead.

THOMYRIS

I am the queen of Scythians.
My strength was like no strength of man's,
  My face like day, my breast like spring.
My fame was felt in the extreme land
That hath sunshine on the one hand
  And on the other star-shining.
Yea, and the wind there fails of breath,
Yea, and there life is waste like death;
  Yea, and there death is a glad thing.

HARHAS

I am the queen of Anakim.
In the spent years whose speech is dim,
  Whose raiment is the dust and death
My stately body without stain
Shone as the shining race of rain
  Whose hair a great wind scattereth,
Now hath God turned my lips to sighs,
Plucked off mine eyelids from mine eyes,
And sealed with seals my way of breath.

MYRRHA

I am the queen Arabian.
The tears wherewith mine eyelids ran
  Smelt like my perfumed eyelids' smell.
A harsh thirst made my soft mouth hard,
That ached with kisses afterward;
  My brain rang like a beaten bell.
As tears on eyes, as fire on wood,
Sin fed upon my breath and blood,
  Sin made my breasts subside and swell.

PASIPHAE

I am the queen Pasiphae.
Not all the pure clean-coloured sea
   Could cleanse or cool my yearning veins;
Nor any root nor herb that grew,
Flag-leaves that let green water through,
   Nor washing of the dews and rains.
From shame's pressed core I wrung the sweet
Fruit's savour that was death to eat,
   Whereof no seed but death remains.

SAPPHO

I am the queen of Lesbians.
My love, that had no part in man's,
   Was sweeter than all shape of sweet.
The intolerable infinite desire
Made my face pale like faded fire
   When the ashen pyre falls through with heat.
My blood was hot wan wine of love,
And my song's sound the sound thereof,
   The sound of the delight of it.

MESSALINA

I am the queen of Italy.
These were the signs God set on me;
   A barren beauty subtle and sleek,
Curled carven hair, and cheeks worn wan
With fierce false lips of many a man,
   Large temples where the blood ran weak,
A mouth athirst and amorous
And hungering as the grave's mouth does
   That, being an-hungred, cannot speak.

AMESTRIS

I am the queen of Persians.
My breasts were lordlier than bright swans,
  My body as amber fair and thin.
Strange flesh was given my lips for bread,
With poisonous hours my days were fed,
  And my feet shod with adder-skin.
In Shushan toward Ecbatane
I wrought my joys with tears and pain,
  My loves with blood and bitter sin.

EPHRATH

I am the queen of Rephaim.
God, that some while refraineth him,
  Made in the end a spoil of me.
My rumour was upon the world
As strong sound of swoln water hurled
  Through porches of the straining sea.
My hair was like the flag-flower,
And my breasts carven goodlier
  Than beryl with chalcedony.

PASITHEA

I am the queen of Cypriotes.
Mine oarsmen, labouring with brown throats,
  Sang of me many a tender thing.
My maidens, girdled loose and braced
With gold from bosom to white waist,
  Praised me between their wool-combing.
All that praise Venus all night long
With lips like speech and lids like song
  Praised me till song lost heart to sing.

146

ALACIEL

I am the queen Alaciel.
My mouth was like that moist gold cell
    Whereout the thickest honey drips.
Mine eyes were as a grey-green sea;
The amorous blood that smote on me
    Smote to my feet and finger-tips.
My throat was whiter than the dove,
Mine eyelids as the seals of love,
    And as the doors of love my lips.

ERIGONE

I am the queen Erigone.
The wild wine shed as blood on me
    Made my face brighter than a bride's.
My large lips had the old thirst of earth,
Mine arms the might of the old sea's girth
    Bound round the whole world's iron sides.
Within mine eyes and in mine ears
Were music and the wine of tears,
    And light, and thunder of the tides.
        Et hìc exeant, et dicat Bersabe regina;

Alas, God, for thy great pity
And for the might that is in thee,
Behold, I woful Bersabe
Cry out with stoopings of my knee
And thy wrath laid and bound on me
    Till I may see thy love.
Behold, Lord, this child is grown
Within me between bone and bone
To make me mother of a son,

Made of my body with strong moan;
There shall not be another one
    That shall be made hereof.

KING DAVID

Lord God, alas, what shall I sain?
Lo, thou art as an hundred men
Both to break and build again:
The wild ways thou makest plain,
Thine hands hold the hail and rain,
And thy fingers both grape and grain;
Of their largess we be all well fain,
    And of their great pity:
The sun thou madest of good gold,
Of clean silver the moon cold,
All the great stars thou hast told
As thy cattle in thy fold
Every one by his name of old;
Wind and water thou hast in hold,
    Both the land and the long sea;
Both the green sea and the land,
Lord God, thou hast in hand,
Both white water and grey sand;
Upon thy right or thy left hand
There is no man that may stand;
    Lord, thou rue on me.
O wise Lord, if thou be keen
To note things amiss that been,
I am not worth a shell of bean
More than an old mare meagre and lean
For all my wrong-doing with my queen,
It grew not of our heartès clean,

But it began of her body.
For it fell in the hot May
I stood within a paven way
Built of fair bright stone, perfay,
That is as fire of night and day
    And lighteth all my house.
Therein be neither stones nor sticks
Neither red nor white bricks,
But for cubits five or six
There is most goodly sardonyx
    And amber laid in rows.
It goes round about my roofs,
(If ye list ye shall have proofs)
There is good space for horse and hoofs,
    Plain and nothing perilous.
For the fair green weather's heat,
And for the smell of leavès sweet,
It is no marvel, well ye weet,
    A man to waxen amorous.
This I say now by my case
That spied forth of that royal place;
There I saw in no great space
Mine own sweet, both body and face,
Under the fresh boughs.
In a water that was there
She wesshe her goodly body bare
And dried it with her owen hair:
Both her arms and her knees fair,
    Both bosom and brows;
Both shoulders and eke thighs
Tho she wesshe upon this wise;
Ever she sighed with little sighs,
    And ever she gave God thank.

Yea, God wot I can well see yet
Both her breast and her sides all wet
And her long hair withouten let
Spread sideways like a drawing net;
Full dear bought and full far fet
Was that sweet thing there y-set;
It were a hard thing to forget
How both lips and eyen met,
   Breast and breath sank.
So goodly a sight as there she was,
Lying looking on her glass
By wan water in green grass,
   Yet saw never man.

So soft and great she was and bright
With all her body waxen white,
I woxe nigh blind to see the light
Shed out of it to left and right;
This bitter sin from that sweet sight
   Between us twain began.

NATHAN

Now, sir, be merry anon,
For ye shall have a full wise son,
Goodly and great of flesh and bone;
There shall no king be such an one,
   I swear by Godis rood.
Therefore, lord, be merry here,
And go to meat withouten fear,
And hear a mass with goodly cheer;
For to all folk ye shall be dear,
   And all folk of your blood.

   Et tunc dicant Laudamus.

ST DOROTHY

It hath been seen and yet it shall be seen
That out of tender mouths God's praise hath been
Made perfect, and with wood and simple string
He hath played music sweet as shawm-playing
To please himself with softness of all sound;
And no small thing but hath been sometime found
Full sweet of use, and no such humbleness
But God hath bruised withal the sentences
And evidence of wise men witnessing;
No leaf that is so soft a hidden thing
It never shall get sight of the great sun;
The strength of ten has been the strength of one,
And lowliness has waxed imperious.
    There was in Rome a man Theophilus
Of right great blood and gracious ways, that had
All noble fashions to make people glad
And a soft life of pleasurable days;
He was a goodly man for one to praise,
Flawless and whole upward from foot to head;
His arms were a red hawk that alway fed
On a small bird with feathers gnawed upon,
Beaten and plucked about the bosom-bone
Whereby a small round fleck like fire there was:
They called it in their tongue lampadias;
This was the banner of the lordly man.
In many straits of sea and reaches wan

Full of quick wind, and many a shaken firth,
It had seen fighting days of either earth,
Westward or east of waters Gaditane
(This was the place of sea-rocks under Spain
Called after the great praise of Hercules)
And north beyond the washing Pontic seas,
Far windy Russian places fabulous,
And salt fierce tides of storm-swol'n Bosphorus.

Now as this lord came straying in Rome town
He saw a little lattice open down
And after it a press of maidens' heads
That sat upon their cold small quiet beds
Talking, and played upon short-stringèd lutes;
And other some ground perfume out of roots
Gathered by marvellous moons in Asia
Saffron and aloes and wild cassia,
Coloured all through and smelling of the sun;
And over all these was a certain one
Clothed softly, with sweet herbs about her hair
And bosom flowerful, her face more fair
Than sudden-singing April in soft lands:
Eyed like a gracious bird, and in both hands
She held a psalter painted green and red.

This Theophile laughed at the heart, and said
Now God so help me hither and St Paul,
As by the new time of their festival
I have good will to take this maid to wife.
And herewith fell to fancies of her life
And soft half-thoughts that ended suddenly.
This is man's guise to please himself, when he
Shall not see one thing of his pleasant things,
Nor with outwatch of many travailings
Come to be eased of the least pain he hath

For all his love and all his foolish wrath
And all the heavy manner of his mind.
Thus is he like a fisher fallen blind
That casts his nets across the boat awry
To strike the sea, but lo, he striketh dry
And plucks them back all broken for his pain
And bites his beard and casts across again
And reaching wrong slips over in the sea.
So hath this man a strangled neck for fee,
For all his cost he chuckles in his throat.
This Theophile that little hereof wote
Laid wait to hear of her what she might be:
Men told him she had name of Dorothy,
And was a lady of a worthy house.
Thereat this knight grew inly glorious
That he should have a love so fair of place.
She was a maiden of most quiet face,
Tender of speech, and had no hardihood
But was nigh feeble of her fearful blood;
Her mercy in her was so marvellous
From her least years, that seeing her school-fellows
That read beside her stricken with a rod,
She would cry sore and say some word to God
That he would ease her fellow of his pain.
There is no touch of sun or fallen rain
That ever fell on a more gracious thing.

   In middle Rome there was in stone-working
The church of Venus painted royally.
The chapels of it were some two or three,
In each of them her tabernacle was
And a wide window of six feet in glass
Coloured with all her works in red and gold.
The altars had bright cloths and cups to hold

The wine of Venus for the services,
Made out of honey and crushed wood-berries
That shed sweet yellow through the thick wet red,
That on high days was borne upon the head
Of Venus' priest for any man to drink;
So that in drinking he should fall to think
On some fair face, and in the thought thereof
Worship, and such should triumph in his love.
For this soft wine that did such grace and good
Was new trans-shaped and mixed with love's own blood,
That in the fighting Trojan time was bled;
For which came such a woe to Diomed
That he was stifled after in hard sea.
And some said that this wine-shedding should be
Made of the falling of Adonis' blood,
That curled upon the thorns and broken wood
And round the gold silk shoes on Venus' feet;
The taste thereof was as hot honey sweet
And in the mouth ran soft and riotous.
This was the holiness of Venus' house.

    It was their worship, that in August days
Twelve maidens should go through those Roman ways
Naked, and having gold across their brows
And their hair twisted in short golden rows,
To minister to Venus in this wise:
And twelve men chosen in their companies
To match these maidens by the altar-stair,
All in one habit, crowned upon the hair.
Among these men was chosen Theophile.

    This knight went out and prayed a little while,
Holding queen Venus by her hands and knees:
I will give thee twelve royal images
Cut in glad gold, with marvels of wrought stone

For thy sweet priests to lean and pray upon,
Jasper and hyacinth and chrysopras,
And the strange Asian thalamite that was
Hidden twelve ages under heavy sea
Among the little sleepy pearls, to be
A shrine lit over with soft candle-flame
Burning all night red as hot brows of shame,
So thou wilt be my lady without sin.
Goddess that art all gold outside and in,
Help me to serve thee in thy holy way.
Thou knowest, Love, that in my bearing day
There shone a laughter in the singing stars
Round the gold-ceilèd bride-bed wherein Mars
Touched thee and had thee in your kissing wise.
Now therefore, sweet, kiss thou my maiden's eyes
That they may open graciously towards me;
And this new fashion of thy shrine shall be
As soft with gold as thine own happy head.
    The goddess, that was painted with face red
Between two long green tumbled sides of sea,
Stooped her neck sideways, and spake pleasantly:
Thou shalt have grace as thou art thrall of mine.
And with this came a savour of shed wine
And plucked-out petals from a rose's head:
And softly with slow laughs of lip she said,
Thou shalt have favour all thy days of me.
    Then came Theophilus to Dorothy,
Saying: O sweet, if one should strive or speak
Against God's ways, he gets a beaten cheek
For all his wage and shame above all men.
Therefore I have no will to turn again
When God saith 'go', lest a worse thing fall out.
Then she, misdoubting lest he went about

To catch her wits, made answer somewhat thus:
I have no will, my lord Theophilus,
To speak against this worthy word of yours;
Knowing how God's will in all speech endures,
That save by grace there may no thing be said.
Then Theophile waxed light from foot to head,
And softly fell upon this answering.
It is well seen you are a chosen thing
To do God service in his gracious way.
I will that you make haste and holiday
To go next year upon the Venus stair,
Covered none else, but crowned upon your hair,
And do the service that a maiden doth.
She said: but I that am Christ's maid were loth
To do this thing that hath such bitter name.
Thereat his brows were beaten with sore shame
And he came off and said no other word.
Then his eyes chanced upon his banner-bird,
And he fell fingering at the staff of it
And laughed for wrath and stared between his feet,
And out of a chafed heart he spake as thus:
Lo, how she japes at me Theophilus,
Feigning herself a fool and hard to love;
Yet in good time for all she boasteth of
She shall be like a little beaten bird.
And while his mouth was open in that word
He came upon the house Janiculum,
Where some went busily, and other some
Talked in the gate called the gate glorious.
The emperor, which was one Gabalus,
Sat over all and drank chill wine alone.
To whom is come Theophilus anon,
And said as thus: *Beau sire, Dieu vous aide.*

And afterward sat under him, and said
All this thing through as ye have wholly heard.
   This Gabalus laughed thickly in his beard.
Yea, this is righteousness and maiden rule.
Truly, he said, a maid is but a fool.
And japed at them as one full villainous,
In a lewd wise, this heathen Gabalus,
And sent his men to bind her as he bade.
Thus have they taken Dorothy the maid,
And haled her forth as men hale pick-purses:
A little need God knows they had of this,
To hale her by her maiden gentle hair.
Thus went she lowly, making a soft prayer,
As one who stays the sweet wine in his mouth,
Murmuring with eased lips, and is most loth
To have done wholly with the sweet of it.
   Christ king, fair Christ, that knowest all men's wit
And all the feeble fashion of my ways,
O perfect God, that from all yesterdays
Abidest whole with morrows perfected,
I pray thee by thy mother's holy head
Thou help me to do right, that I not slip:
I have no speech nor strength upon my lip,
Except thou help me who art wise and sweet.
Do this too for those nails that clove thy feet,
Let me die maiden after many pains.
Though I be least among thy handmaidens,
Doubtless I shall take death more sweetly thus.
   Now have they brought her to King Gabalus,
Who laughed in all his throat some breathing-whiles.
By God, he said, if one should leap two miles,
He were not pained about the sides so much.
This were a soft thing for a man to touch.

Shall one so chafe that hath such little bones?
And shook his throat with thick and chuckled moans
For laughter that she had such holiness.
What aileth thee, wilt thou do services?
It were good fare to fare as Venus doth.

Then said this lady with her maiden mouth,
Shamefaced, and something paler in the cheek:
Now, sir, albeit my wit and will to speak
Give me no grace in sight of worthy men,
For all my shame yet know I this again,
I may not speak, nor after downlying
Rise up to take delight in lute-playing,
Nor sing nor sleep, nor sit and fold my hands,
But my soul in some measure understands
God's grace laid like a garment over me.
For this fair God that out of strong sharp sea
Lifted the shapely and green-coloured land,
And hath the weight of heaven in his hand
As one might hold a bird, and under him
The heavy golden planets beam by beam
Building the feasting-chambers of his house,
And the large world he holdeth with his brows,
And with the light of them astonisheth
All place and time and face of life and death
And motion of the north wind and the south,
And is the sound within his angel's mouth
Of singing words and words of thanksgiving,
And is the colour of the latter spring
And heat upon the summer and the sun,
And is beginning of all things begun
And gathers in him all things to their end,
And with the fingers of his hand doth bend
The stretched-out sides of heaven like a sail,

And with his breath he maketh the red pale
And fills with blood faint faces of men dead,
And with the sound between his lips are fed
Iron and fire and the white body of snow,
And blossom of all trees in places low,
And small bright herbs about the little hills,
And fruit pricked softly with birds' tender bills,
And flight of foam about green fields of sea,
And fourfold strength of the great winds that be
Moved always outward from beneath his feet,
And growth of grass and growth of sheavèd wheat
And all green flower of goodly-growing lands;
And all these things he gathers with his hands
And covers all their beauty with his wings;
The same, even God that governs all these things,
Hath set my feet to be upon his ways.
Now therefore for no painfulness of days
I shall put off this service bound on me.
Also, fair sir, ye know this certainly,
How God was in his flesh full chaste and meek
And gave his face to shame, and either cheek
Gave up to smiting of men tyrannous.
    And here with a great voice this Gabalus
Cried out and said: By God's blood and his bones,
This were good game betwixen night and nones
For one to sit and hearken to such saws:
I were as lief fall in some big beast's jaws
As hear these women's jaw-teeth chattering,
By God a woman is the harder thing,
One may not put a hook into her mouth.
Now by St Luke I am so sore adrouth
For all these saws I must needs drink again:
But I pray God deliver all us men

From all such noise of women and their heat.
That is a noble scripture, well I weet,
That likens women to an empty can;
When God said that he was a full wise man.
I trow no man may blame him as for that.
    And herewithal he drank a draught, and spat,
And said: Now shall I make an end hereof.
Come near all men and hearken for God's love,
And ye shall hear a jest or twain, God wot.
And spake as thus with mouth full thick and hot;
But thou do this thou shalt be shortly slain.
Lo, sir, she said, this death and all this pain
I take in penance of my bitter sins.
Yea, now, quoth Gabalus, this game begins.
Lo, without sin one shall not live a span.
Lo, this is she that would not look on man
Between her fingers folded in thwart wise.
See how her shame hath smitten in her eyes
That was so clean she had not heard of shame.
Certes, he said, by Gabalus my name,
This two years back I was not so well pleased.
This were good mirth for sick men to be eased
And rise up whole and laugh at hearing of.
I pray thee show us something of thy love,
Since thou wast maid thy gown is waxen wide.
Yea, maid I am, she said, and somewhat sighed,
As one who thought upon the low fair house
Where she sat working, with soft bended brows
Watching her threads, among the school-maidens.
And she thought well now God had brought her thence
She should not come to sew her gold again.
    Then cried King Gabalus upon his men
To have her forth and draw her with steel gins.

And as a man hag-ridden beats and grins
And bends his body sidelong in his bed,
So wagged he with his body and knave's head,
Gaping at her, and blowing with his breath.
And in good time he gat an evil death
Out of his lewdness with his cursèd wives:
His bones were hewn asunder as with knives
For his misliving, certes it is said.
But all the evil wrought upon this maid,
It were full hard for one to handle it.
For her soft blood was shed upon her feet,
And all her body's colour bruised and faint.
But she, as one abiding God's great saint,
Spake not nor wept for all this travail hard.
Wherefore the king commanded afterward
To slay her presently in all men's sight.
And it was now an hour upon the night
And winter-time, and a few stars began.
The weather was yet feeble and all wan
For beating of a weighty wind and snow.
And she came walking in soft wise and slow,
And many men with faces piteous.
Then came this heavy cursing Gabalus,
That swore full hard into his drunken beard;
And faintly after without any word
Came Theophile some paces off the king.
And in the middle of this wayfaring
Full tenderly beholding her he said:

There is no word of comfort with men dead
Nor any face and colour of things sweet;
But always with lean cheeks and lifted feet
These dead men lie all aching to the blood
With bitter cold, their brows withouten hood

Beating for chill, their bodies swathed full thin.
Alas, what hire shall any have herein
To give his life and get such bitterness?
Also the soul going forth bodiless
Is hurt with naked cold, and no man saith
If there be house or covering for death
To hide the soul that is discomforted.
    Then she beholding him a little said:
Alas, fair lord, ye have no wit of this;
For on one side death is full poor of bliss
And as ye say full sharp of bone and lean:
But on the other side is good and green
And hath soft flower of tender-coloured hair
Grown on his head, and a red mouth as fair
As may be kissed with lips; thereto his face
Is as God's face, and in a perfect place
Full of all sun and colour of straight boughs
And waterheads about a painted house
That hath a mile of flowers either way
Outward from it, and blossom-grass of May
Thickening on many a side for length of heat,
Hath God set death upon a noble seat
Covered with green and flowered in the fold,
In likeness of a great king grown full old
And gentle with new temperance of blood;
And on his brows a purfled purple hood,
They may not carry any golden thing;
And plays some tune with subtle fingering
On a small cithern, full of tears and sleep
And heavy pleasure that is quick to weep
And sorrow with the honey in her mouth;
And for this might of music that he doth
Are all souls drawn toward him with great love

And weep for sweetness of the noise thereof
And bow to him with worship of their knees;
And all the field is thick with companies
Of fair-clothed men that play on shawms and lutes
And gather honey of the yellow fruits
Between the branches waxen soft and wide:
And all this peace endures in either side
Of the green land, and God beholdeth all.
And this is girdled with a round fair wall
Made of red stone and cool with heavy leaves
Grown out against it, and green blossom cleaves
To the green chinks, and lesser wall-weed sweet,
Kissing the crannies that are split with heat,
And branches where the summer draws to head.

    And Theophile burnt in the cheek, and said:
Yea, could one see it, this were marvellous.
I pray you, at your coming to this house,
Give me some leaf of all those tree-branches;
Seeing how so sharp and white our weather is,
There is no green nor gracious red to see.

    Yea, sir, she said, that shall I certainly.
And from her long sweet throat without a fleck
Undid the gold, and through her stretched-out neck
The cold axe clove, and smote away her head:
Out of her throat the tender blood full red
Fell suddenly through all her long soft hair.
And with good speed for hardness of the air
Each man departed to his house again.

    Lo, as fair colour in the face of men
At seed-time of their blood, or in such wise
As a thing seen increaseth in men's eyes,
Caught first far off by sickly fits of sight—
So a word said, if one shall hear aright,

Abides against the season of its growth.
This Theophile went slowly, as one doth
That is not sure for sickness of his feet;
And counting the white stonework of the street,
Tears fell out of his eyes for wrath and love,
Making him weep more for the shame thereof
Than for true pain: so went he half a mile.
And women mocked him, saying: Theophile,
Lo, she is dead, what shall a woman have
That loveth such an one? so Christ me save,
I were as lief to love a man new-hung.
Surely this man has bitten on his tongue,
This makes him sad and writhled in his face.
   And when they came upon the paven place
That was called sometime the place amorous
There came a child before Theophilus
Bearing a basket, and said suddenly:
Fair sir, this is my mistress Dorothy
That sends you gifts; and with this he was gone.
In all this earth there is not such an one
For colour and straight stature made so fair.
The tender growing gold of his pure hair
Was as wheat growing, and his mouth as flame.
God called him Holy after his own name;
With gold cloth like fire burning he was clad.
But for the fair green basket that he had,
It was filled up with heavy white and red;
Great roses stained still where the first rose bled,
Burning at heart for shame their heart withholds:
And the sad colour of strong marigolds
That have the sun to kiss their lips for love;
The flower that Venus' hair is woven of,
The colour of fair apples in the sun,

Late peaches gathered when the heat was done
And the slain air got breath; and after these
The fair faint-headed poppies drunk with ease,
And heaviness of hollow lilies red.
   Then cried they all that saw these things, and said
It was God's doing, and was marvellous.
And in brief while this knight Theophilus
Is waxen full of faith, and witnesseth
Before the king of God and love and death,
For which the king bade hang him presently.
A gallows of a goodly piece of tree
This Gabalus hath made to hang him on.
Forth of this world lo Theophile is gone
With a wried neck, God give us better fare
Than his that hath a twisted throat to wear;
But truly for his love God that him brought
There where his heavy body grieves him nought
Nor all the people plucking at his feet;
But in his face his lady's face is sweet,
And through his lips her kissing lips are gone:
God send him peace, and joy of such an one.
   This is the story of St Dorothy.
I will you of your mercy pray for me
Because I wrote these sayings for your grace,
That I may one day see her in the face.

THE TWO DREAMS

(From Boccaccio)

I will that if I say a heavy thing
Your tongues forgive me; seeing ye know that spring
Has flecks and fits of pain to keep her sweet,
And walks somewhile with winter-bitten feet.
Moreover it sounds often well to let
One string, when ye play music, keep at fret
The whole song through; one petal that is dead
Confirms the roses, be they white or red;
Dead sorrow is not sorrowful to hear
As the thick noise that breaks mid weeping were;
The sick sound aching in a lifted throat
Turns to sharp silver of a perfect note;
And though the rain falls often, and with rain
Late autumn falls on the old red leaves like pain,
I deem that God is not disquieted.
Also while men are fed with wine and bread,
They shall be fed with sorrow at his hand.
   There grew a rose-garden in Florence land
More fair than many; all red summers through
The leaves smelt sweet and sharp of rain, and blew
Sideways with tender wind; and therein fell
Sweet sound wherewith the green waxed audible,
As a bird's will to sing disturbed his throat
And set the sharp wings forward like a boat

Pushed through soft water, moving his brown side
Smooth-shapen as a maid's, and shook with pride
His deep warm bosom, till the heavy sun's
Set face of heat stopped all the songs at once.
The ways were clean to walk and delicate;
And when the windy white of March grew late,
Before the trees took heart to face the sun
With ravelled raiment of lean winter on,
The roots were thick and hot with hollow grass.
  Some roods away a lordly house there was,
Cool with broad courts and latticed passage wet
From rush-flowers and lilies ripe to set,
Sown close among the strewings of the floor;
And either wall of the slow corridor
Was dim with deep device of gracious things;
Some angel's steady mouth and weight of wings
Shut to the side; or Peter with straight stole
And beard cut black against the aureole
That spanned his head from nape to crown; thereby
Mary's gold hair, thick to the girdle-tie
Wherein was bound a child with tender feet;
Or the broad cross with blood nigh brown on it.
  Within this house a righteous lord abode,
Ser Averardo; patient of his mood,
And just of judgment; and to child he had
A maid so sweet that her mere sight made glad
Men sorrowing, and unbound the brows of hate;
And where she came, the lips that pain made strait
Waxed warm and wide, and from untender grew
Tender as those that sleep brings patience to.
Such long locks had she, that with knee to chin
She might have wrapped and warmed her feet therein.
Right seldom fell her face on weeping wise;

Gold hair she had, and golden-coloured eyes,
Filled with clear light and fire and large repose
Like a fair hound's; no man there is but knows
Her face was white, and thereto she was tall;
In no wise lacked there any praise at all
To her most perfect and pure maidenhood;
No sin I think there was in all her blood.

　　She, where a gold grate shut the roses in,
Dwelt daily through deep summer weeks, through green
Flushed hours of rain upon the leaves; and there
Love made him room and space to worship her
With tender worship of bowed knees, and wrought
Such pleasure as the pained sense palates not
For weariness, but at one taste undoes
The heart of its strong sweet, is ravenous
Of all the hidden honey; words and sense
Fail through the tune's imperious prevalence.

　　In a poor house this lover kept apart,
Long communing with patience next his heart
If love of his might move that face at all,
Tuned evenwise with colours musical;
Then after length of days he said thus: 'Love,
For love's own sake and for the love thereof
Let no harsh words untune your gracious mood;
For good it were, if anything be good,
To comfort me in this pain's plague of mine;
Seeing thus, how neither sleep nor bread nor wine
Seems pleasant to me, yea, no thing that is
Seems pleasant to me; only I know this,
Love's ways are sharp for palms of piteous feet
To travel, but the end of such is sweet:
Now do with me as seemeth you the best.'
She mused a little, as one holds his guest

By the hand musing, with her face borne down:
Then said: 'Yea, though such bitter seed be sown
Have no more care of all that you have said;
Since if there is no sleep will bind your head,
Lo, I am fain to help you certainly;
Christ knoweth, sir, if I would have you die;
There is no pleasure when a man is dead.'
Thereat he kissed her hands and yellow head
And clipped her fair long body many times;
I have no wit to shape in written rhymes
A scanted tithe of this great joy they had.

   They were too near love's secret to be glad
As whoso deems the core will surely melt
From the warm fruit his lips caress, hath felt
Some bitter kernel where the teeth shut hard:
Or as sweet music sharpens afterward.
Being half disrelished both for sharp and sweet;
As sea-water, having killed over-heat
In a man's body, chills it with faint ache;
So their sense, burdened only for love's sake,
Failed for pure love; yet so time served their wit.
They saved each day some gold reserves of it,
Being wiser in love's riddle than such be
Whom fragments feed with his chance charity.
All things felt sweet were felt sweet overmuch;
The rose-thorn's prickle dangerous to touch,
And flecks of fire in the thin leaf-shadows;
Too keen the breathèd honey of the rose,
Its red too harsh a weight on feasted eyes;
They were so far gone in love's histories,
Beyond all shape and colour and mere breath,
Where pleasure has for kinsfolk sleep and death,
And strength of soul and body waxen blind

M   169

For weariness, and flesh entoiled with mind,
When the keen edge of sense foretasteth sin.
   Even this green place the summer caught them in
Seemed half deflowered and sick with beaten leaves
In their strayed eyes; these gold flower-fumèd eves
Burnt out to make the sun's love-offering,
The midnoon's prayer, the rose's thanksgiving,
The trees' weight burdening the strengthless air,
The shape of her stilled eyes, her coloured hair,
Her body's balance from the moving feet—
All this, found fair, lacked yet one grain of sweet
It had some warm weeks back: so perisheth
On May's new lip the tender April breath:
So those same walks the wind sowed lilies in
All April through, and all their latter kin
Of languid leaves whereon the Autumn blows—
The dead red raiment of the last year's rose—
The last year's laurel, and the last year's love,
Fade, and grow things that death grows weary of.
   What man will gather in red summer-time
The fruit of some obscure and hoary rhyme
Heard last midwinter, taste the heart in it,
Mould the smooth semitones afresh, refit
The fair limbs ruined, flush the dead blood through
With colour, make all broken beauties new
For love's new lesson—shall not such find pain
When the marred music labouring in his brain
Frets him with sweet sharp fragments, and lets slip
One word that might leave satisfied his lip—
One touch that might put fire in all the chords?
This was her pain: to miss from all sweet words
Some taste of sound, diverse and delicate—
Some speech the old love found out to compensate

For seasons of shut lips and drowsiness—
Some grace, some word the old love found out to bless
Passionless months and undelighted weeks.
The flowers had lost their summer scented cheeks,
Their lips were no more sweet than daily breath:
The year was plagued with instances of death.

　　So fell it, these were sitting in cool grass
With leaves about, and many a bird there was
Where the green shadow thickliest impleached
Soft fruit and writhen spray and blossom bleached
Dry in the sun or washed with rains to white:
Her girdle was pure silk, the bosom bright
With purple as purple water and gold wrought in.
One branch had touched with dusk her lips and chin,
Made violet of the throat, abashed with shade
The breast's bright plaited work: but nothing frayed
The sun's large kiss on the luxurious hair.
Her beauty was new colour to the air,
And music to the silent many birds.
Love was an-hungred for some perfect words
To praise her with; but only her low name
'Andrevuola' came thrice, and thrice put shame
In her clear cheek, so fruitful with new red
That for pure love straightway shame's self was dead.

　　Then with lids gathered as who late had wept
She began saying: 'I have so little slept
My lids drowse now against the very sun;
Yea, the brain aching with a dream begun
Beats like a fitful blood; kiss but both brows,
And you shall pluck my thoughts grown dangerous
Almost away.' He said thus, kissing them:
'O sole sweet thing that God is glad to name,
My one gold gift, if dreams be sharp and sore

Shall not the waking time increase much more
With taste and sound, sweet eyesight or sweet scent?
Has any heat too hard and insolent
Burnt bare the tender married leaves, undone
The maiden grass shut under from the sun?
Where in this world is room enough for pain?'
    The feverish finger of love had touched again
Her lips with happier blood; the pain lay meek
In her fair face, nor altered lip nor cheek
With pallor or with pulse; but in her mouth
Love thirsted as a man wayfaring doth,
Making it humble as weak hunger is.
She lay close to him, bade do this and this,
Say that, sing thus: then almost weeping-ripe
Crouched, then laughed low. As one that fain would wipe
The old record out of old things done and dead,
She rose, she heaved her hands up, and waxed red
For wilful heart and blameless fear of blame;
Saying 'Though my wits be weak, this is no shame
For a poor maid whom love so punisheth
With heats of hesitation and stopped breath
That with my dreams I live yet heavily
For pure sad heart and faith's humility.
Now be not wroth and I will shew you this.
  'Methought our lips upon their second kiss
Met in this place, and a fair day we had
And fair soft leaves that waxed and were not sad
With shaken rain or bitten through with drouth;
When I, beholding ever how your mouth
Waited for mine, the throat being fallen back,
Saw crawl thereout a live thing flaked with black
Specks of brute slime and leper-coloured scale,
A devil's hide with foul flame-writhen grail

172

Fashioned where hell's heat festers loathsomest;
And that brief speech may ease me of the rest,
Thus were you slain and eaten of the thing.
My waked eyes felt the new day shuddering
On their low lids, felt the whole east so beat,
Pant with close pulse of such a plague-struck heat,
As if the palpitating dawn drew breath
For horror, breathing between life and death,
Till the sun sprang blood-bright and violent.'
So finishing, her soft strength wholly spent,
She gazed each way, lest some brute-hoovèd thing,
The timeless travail of hell's childbearing,
Should threat upon the sudden: whereat he,
For relish of her tasted misery
And tender little thornprick of her pain,
Laughed with mere love. What lover among men
But hath his sense fed sovereignly 'twixt whiles
With tears and covered eyelids and sick smiles
And soft disaster of a painèd face?
What pain, established in so sweet a place,
But the plucked leaf of it smells fragrantly?
What colour burning man's wide-open eye
But may be pleasurably seen? what sense
Keeps in its hot sharp extreme violence
No savour of sweet things? The bereaved blood
And emptied flesh in their most broken mood
Fail not so wholly, famish not when thus
Past honey keeps the starved lip covetous.
Therefore this speech from a glad mouth began,
Breathed in her tender hair and temples wan
Like one prolonged kiss while the lips had breath:
'Sleep, that abides in vassalage of death
And in death's service wears out half his age,

173

Hath his dreams full of deadly vassalage,
Shadow and sound of things ungracious;
Fair shallow faces, hooded bloodless brows,
And mouths past kissing; yea, myself have had
As harsh a dream as holds your eyelids sad.
   'This dream I tell you came three nights ago;
In full mid sleep I took a whim to know
How sweet things might be, so I turned and thought;
But save my dream all sweet availed me not.
First came a smell of pounded spice and scent
Such as God ripens in some continent
Of utmost amber in the Syrian sea;
And breaths as though some costly rose could be
Spoiled slowly, wasted by some bitter fire
To burn the sweet out leaf by leaf, and tire
The flower's poor heart with heat and waste, to make
Strong magic for some perfumed woman's sake.
Then a cool naked sense beneath my feet
Of bud and blossom; and sound of veins that beat
As if a lute should play of its own heart
And fearfully, not smitten of either part;
And all my blood it filled with sharp and sweet
As gold swoln grain fills out the huskèd wheat;
So I rose naked from the bed, and stood
Counting the mobile measure in my blood
Some pleasant while, and through each limb there came
Swift little pleasures pungent as a flame,
Felt in the thrilling flesh and veins as much
As the outer curls that feel the comb's first touch
Thrill to the roots and shiver as from fire;
And blind between my dream and my desire
I seemed to stand and held my spirit still
Lest this should cease. A child whose fingers spill

Honey from cells forgotten of the bee
Is less afraid to stir the hive and see
Some wasp's bright back inside, than I to feel
Some finger-touch disturb the flesh like steel.
I prayed thus; Let me catch a secret here
So sweet, it sharpens the sweet taste of fear
And takes the mouth with edge of wine; I would
Have here some colour and smooth shape as good
As those in heaven whom the chief garden hides
With low grape-blossom veiling their white sides
And lesser tendrils that so bind and blind
Their eyes and feet, that if one come behind
To touch their hair they see not, neither fly;
This would I see in heaven and not die.
So praying, I had nigh cried out and knelt,
So wholly my prayer filled me: till I felt
In the dumb night's warm weight of glowing gloom
Somewhat that altered all my sleeping-room
And made it like a green low place wherein
Maids mix to bathe: one sets her small warm chin
Against a ripple, that the angry pearl
May flow like flame about her: the next curl
Dips in some eddy coloured of the sun
To wash the dust well out; another one
Holds a straight ankle in her hand and swings
With lavish body sidelong, so that rings
Of sweet fierce water, swollen and splendid, fail
All round her fine and floated body pale,
Swayed flower-fashion, and her balanced side
Swerved edgeways lets the weight of water slide,
As taken in some underflow of sea
Swerves the banked gold of sea-flowers; but she
Pulls down some branch to keep her perfect head

Clear of the river: even from wall to bed,
I tell you, was my room transfigured so.
Sweet, green and warm it was, nor could one know
If there were walls or leaves, or if there was
No bed's green curtain, but mere gentle grass.
There were set also hard against the feet
Gold plates with honey and green grapes to eat,
With the cool water's noise to hear in rhymes:
And a wind warmed me full of furze and limes
And all hot sweets the heavy summer fills
To the round brim of smooth cup-shapen hills.
Next the grave walking of a woman's feet
Made my veins hesitate, and gracious heat
Made thick the lids and leaden on mine eyes:
And I thought ever, surely it were wise
Not yet to see her: this may last (who knows?)
Five minutes; the poor rose is twice a rose
Because it turns a face to her, the wind
Sings that way; hath this woman ever sinned,
I wonder? as a boy with apple-rind,
I played with pleasures, made them to my mind,
Changed each ere tasting. When she came indeed
First her hair touched me, then I grew to feed
On the sense of her hand; her mouth at last
Touched me between the cheek and lip and past
Over my face with kisses here and there
Sown in and out across the eyes and hair.
Still I said nothing; till she set her face
More close and harder on the kissing-place,
And her mouth caught like a snake's mouth, and stung
So faint and tenderly, the fang scarce clung
More than a bird's foot: yet a wound it grew,
A great one, let this red mark witness you

Under the left breast; and the stroke thereof
So clove my sense that I woke out of love
And knew not what this dream was nor had wit;
But now God knows if I have skill of it.'
   Hereat she laid one palm against her lips
To stop their trembling; as when water slips
Out of a beak-mouthed vessel with faint noise
And chuckles in the narrowed throat and cloys
The carven rims with murmuring, so came
Words in her lips with no word right of them,
A beaten speech thick and disconsolate,
Till his smile ceasing waxed compassionate
Of her sore fear that grew from anything—
The sound of the strong summer thickening
In heated leaves of the smooth apple-trees:
The day's breath felt about the ash-branches,
And noises of the noon whose weight still grew
On the hot heavy-headed flowers, and drew
Their red mouths open till the rose-heart ached;
For eastward all the crowding rose was slaked
And soothed with shade: but westward all its growth
Seemed to breathe hard with heat as a man doth
Who feels his temples newly feverous.
And even with such motion in her brows
As that man hath in whom sick days begin,
She turned her throat and spake, her voice being thin
As a sick man's, sudden and tremulous;
'Sweet, if this end be come indeed on us,
Let us love more'; and held his mouth with hers.
As the first sound of flooded hill-waters
Is heard by people of the meadow-grass,
Or ever a wandering waif of ruin pass
With whirling stones and foam of the brown stream

Flaked with fierce yellow: so beholding him
She felt before tears came her eyelids wet,
Saw the face deadly thin where life was yet,
Heard his throat's harsh last moan before it clomb:
And he, with close mouth passionate and dumb,
Burned at her lips: so lay they without speech,
Each grasping other, and the eyes of each
Fed in the other's face: till suddenly
He cried out with a little broken cry
This word, 'O help me, sweet, I am but dead.'
And even so saying, the colour of fair red
Was gone out of his face, and his blood's beat
Fell, and stark death made sharp his upward feet
And pointed hands: and without moan he died.
Pain smote her sudden in the brows and side,
Strained her lips open and made burn her eyes:
For the pure sharpness of her miseries
She had no heart's pain, but mere body's wrack,
But at the last her beaten blood drew back
Slowly upon her face, and her stunned brows
Suddenly grown aware and piteous
Gathered themselves, her eyes shone, her hard breath
Came as though one nigh dead came back from death;
Her lips throbbed, and life trembled through her hair.
    And in brief while she thought to bury there
The dead man that her love might lie with him
In a sweet bed under the rose-roots dim
And soft earth round the branchèd apple-trees,
Full of hushed heat and heavy with great ease,
And no man entering divide him thence.
Wherefore she bade one of her handmaidens
To be her help to do upon this wise.
And saying so the tears out of her eyes

Fell without noise and comforted her heart:
Yea, her great pain eased of the sorest part
Began to soften in her sense of it.
There under all the little branches sweet
The place was shapen of his burial;
They shed thereon no thing funereal,
But coloured leaves of latter rose-blossom,
Stems of soft grass, some withered red and some
Fair and flesh-blooded; and spoil splendider
Of marigold and great spent sunflower.
   And afterward she came back without word
To her own house; two days went, and the third
Went, and she showed her father of this thing.
And for great grief of her soul's travailing
He gave consent she should endure in peace
Till her life's end; yea, till her time should cease,
She should abide in fellowship of pain.
And having lived a holy year or twain
She died of pure waste heart and weariness.
And for love's honour in her love's distress
This word was written over her tomb's head:
'Here dead she lieth, for whose sake Love is dead.'

THE YEAR OF LOVE

There were four loves that one by one,
Following the seasons and the sun,
Passed over without tears, and fell
Away without farewell.

The first was made of gold and tears,
The next of aspen-leaves and fears,
The third of rose-boughs and rose-roots,
The last love of strange fruits.

These were the four loves faded. Hold
Some minutes fast the time of gold
When our lips each way clung and clove
To a face full of love.

The tears inside our eyelids met,
Wrung forth with kissing, and wept wet
The faces cleaving each to each
Where the blood served for speech.

The second, with low patient brows
Bound under aspen-coloured boughs
And eyes made strong and grave with sleep
And yet too weak to weep—

The third, with eager mouth at ease
Fed from late autumn honey, lees
Of scarce gold left in latter cells
With scattered flower-smells—

Hair sprinkled over with spoilt sweet
Of ruined roses, wrists and feet
Slight-swathed, as grassy girdled sheaves
Hold in stray poppy-leaves—

The fourth, with lips whereon has bled
Some great pale fruit's slow colour, shed
From the rank bitter husk whence drips
Faint blood between her lips—

Made of the heat of whole great Junes
Burning the blue dark round their moons
(Each like a mown red marigold)
So hard the flame keeps hold—

These are burnt thoroughly away.
Only the first holds out a day
Beyond these latter loves that were
Made of mere heat and air.

And now the time is winterly
The first love fades too: none will see,
When April warms the world anew,
The place wherein love grew.

ESTRILD'S SONG

'Had I wist, quoth Spring to the swallow,
That earth could forget me, kissed
By summer and lured to follow
Down ways that I know not, I,
My heart would have waxed not high,
Mid-March would have seen me die—
Had I wist.'

'Had I wist, O Spring, said the swallow,
That hope was a sunlit mist,
And the faint light heart of it hollow,
Thy woods had not heard me sing,
Thy winds had not known my wing—
It had failed ere thine did, Spring,
Had I wist.'

TRIADS

I

The word of the sun to the sky,
  The word of the wind to the sea,
    The word of the moon to the night,
      What may it be?

II

The sense to the flower of the fly,
  The sense of the bird to the tree,
    The sense to the cloud of the light,
      Who can tell me?

III

The song of the fields to the kye,
  The song of the lime to the bee,
    The song of the depth to the height,
      Who knows all three?

A LYKE-WAKE SONG

Fair of face, full of pride,
Sit ye down by a dead man's side.

Ye sang songs a' the day:
Sit down at night in the red worm's way.

Proud ye were a' day long:
Ye'll be but lean at evensong.

Ye had gowd kells on your hair:
Nae man kens what ye were.

Ye set scorn by the silken stuff:
Now the grave is clean enough.

Ye set scorn by the rubis ring:
Now the worm is a saft sweet thing.

Fine gold and blithe fair face,
Ye are come to a grimly place.

Gold hair and glad grey een,
Nae man kens if ye have been.

SESTINA

I saw my soul at rest upon a day
  As a bird sleeping in the nest of night,
Among soft leaves that give the starlight way
  To touch its wings but not its eyes with light
So that it knew as one in visions may,
  And knew not as men waking, of delight.

This was the measure of my soul's delight;
  It had no power of joy to fly by day,
Nor part in the large lordship of the light;
  But in a secret moon-beholden way
Had all its will of dreams and pleasant night,
  And all the love and life that sleepers may.

But such life's triumph as men waking may
  It might not have to feed its faint delight
Between the stars by night and sun by day,
  Shut up with green leaves and a little light;
Because its way was as a lost star's way,
  A world's not wholly known of day or night.

All loves and dreams and sounds and gleams of night
  Made it all music that such minstrels may,
And all they had they gave it of delight;
  But in the full face of the fire of day
What place shall be for any starry light,
  What part of heaven in all the wide sun's way?

Yet the soul woke not, sleeping by the way,
  Watched as a nursling of the large-eyed night,
And sought no strength nor knowledge of the day,
  Nor closer touch conclusive of delight,
Nor mightier joy nor truer than dreamers may,
  Nor more of song than they, nor more of light.

For who sleeps once and sees the secret light
  Whereby sleep shows the soul a fairer way
Between the rise and rest of day and night,
  Shall care no more to fare as all men may,
But be his place of pain or of delight,
  There shall he dwell, beholding night as day.

Song, have thy day and take thy fill of light
  Before the night be fallen across thy way;
Sing while he may, man hath no long delight.

AVE ATQUE VALE

IN MEMORY OF CHARLES BAUDELAIRE

Nous devrions pourtant lui porter quelques fleurs,
Les morts, les pauvres morts, ont de grandes douleurs,
Et quand Octobre souffle, émondeur des vieux arbres,
Son vent mélancolique à l'entour de leurs marbres,
Certes, ils doivent trouver les vivants bien ingrats.

LES FLEURS DU MAL

I

Shall I strew on thee rose or rue or laurel,
  Brother, on this that was the veil of thee?
  Or quiet sea-flower moulded by the sea,
Or simplest growth of meadow-sweet or sorrel,
  Such as the summer-sleepy Dryads weave,
  Waked up by snow-soft sudden rains at eve?
Or wilt thou rather, as on earth before,
  Half-faded fiery blossoms, pale with heat
  And full of bitter summer, but more sweet
To thee than gleanings of a northern shore
  Trod by no tropic feet?

II

For always thee the fervid languid glories
  Allured of heavier suns in mightier skies;
  Thine ears knew all the wandering watery sighs
Where the sea sobs round Lesbian promontories,

The barren kiss of piteous wave to wave
  That knows not where is that Leucadian grave
Which hides too deep the supreme head of song.
  Ah, salt and sterile as her kisses were,
  The wild sea winds her and the green gulfs bear
Hither and thither, and vex and work her wrong,
  Blind gods that cannot spare.

III

Thou sawest, in thine old singing season, brother,
  Secrets and sorrows unbeheld of us:
  Fierce loves, and lovely leaf-buds poisonous,
Bare to thy subtler eye, but for none other
Blowing by night in some unbreathed-in clime;
  The hidden harvest of luxurious time,
Sin without shape, and pleasure without speech;
  And where strange dreams in a tumultuous sleep
  Make the shut eyes of stricken spirits weep;
And with each face thou sawest the shadow on each,
Seeing as men sow men reap.

IV

O sleepless heart and sombre soul unsleeping,
  That were athirst for sleep and no more life
  And no more love, for peace and no more strife!
Now the dim gods of death have in their keeping
  Spirit and body and all the springs of song,
  Is it well now where love can do no wrong,
Where stingless pleasure has no foam or fang
  Behind the unopening closure of her lips?
  Is it not well where soul from body slips
And flesh from bone divides without a pang
  As dew from flower-bell drips?

V

It is enough, the end and the beginning
    Are one thing to thee, who art past the end.
    O hand unclasped of unbeholden friend,
For thee no fruits to pluck, no palms for winning,
    No triumph and no labour and no lust,
    Only dead yew-leaves and a little dust.
O quiet eyes wherein the light saith nought,
    Whereto the day is dumb, nor any night
    With obscure finger silences your sight,
Nor in your speech the sudden soul speaks thought,
    Sleep, and have sleep for light.

VI

Now all strange hours and all strange loves are over,
    Dreams and desires and sombre songs and sweet,
    Hast thou found place at the great knees and feet
Of some pale Titan-woman like a lover,
    Such as thy vision here solicited,
    Under the shadow of her fair vast head,
The deep division of prodigious breasts,
    The solemn slope of mighty limbs asleep,
    The weight of awful tresses that still keep
The savour and shade of old-world pine-forests
    Where the wet hill-winds weep?

VII

Hast thou found any likeness for thy vision?
    O gardener of strange flowers, what bud, what bloom,
    Hast thou found sown, what gathered in the gloom?
What of despair, of rapture, of derision,
    What of life is there, what of ill or good?
    Are the fruits grey like dust or bright like blood?

Does the dim ground grow any seed of ours,
    The faint fields quicken any terrene root,
    In low lands where the sun and moon are mute
And all the stars keep silence? Are there flowers
    At all, or any fruit?

VIII

Alas, but though my flying song flies after,
    O sweet strange elder singer, thy more fleet
    Singing, and footprints of thy fleeter feet,
Some dim derision of mysterious laughter
    From the blind tongueless warders of the dead,
    Some gainless glimpse of Proserpine's veiled head,
Some little sound of unregarded tears
    Wept by effaced unprofitable eyes,
    And from pale mouths some cadence of dead sighs—
These only, these the hearkening spirit hears,
    Sees only such things rise.

IX

Thou art far too far for wings of words to follow,
    Far too far off for thought or any prayer.
    What ails us with thee, who art wind and air?
What ails us gazing where all seen is hollow?
    Yet with some fancy, yet with some desire,
    Dreams pursue death as winds a flying fire,
Our dreams pursue our dead and do not find.
    Still, and more swift than they, the thin flame flies
    The low light fails us in elusive skies,
Still the foiled earnest ear is deaf, and blind
    Are still the eluded eyes.

X

Not thee, O never thee, in all time's changes,
  Not thee, but this the sound of thy sad soul,
  The shadow of thy swift spirit, this shut scroll
I lay my hand on, and not death estranges
  My spirit from communion of thy song—
  These memories and these melodies that throng
Veiled porches of a Muse funereal—
  These I salute, these touch, these clasp and fold
  As though a hand were in my hand to hold,
Or through mine ears a mourning musical
  Of many mourners rolled.

XI

I among these, I also, in such station
  As when the pyre was charred, and piled the sods,
  And offering to the dead made, and their gods,
The old mourners had, standing to make libation,
  I stand, and to the gods and to the dead
  Do reverence without prayer or praise, and shed
Offering to these unknown, the gods of gloom,
  And what of honey and spice my seedlands bear,
  And what I may of fruits in this chilled air,
And lay, Orestes-like, across the tomb
  A curl of severed hair.

XII

But by no hand nor any treason stricken,
  Not like the low-lying head of Him, the King,
  The flame that made of Troy a ruinous thing,
Thou liest and on this dust no tears could quicken
There fall no tears like theirs that all men hear
  Fall tear by sweet imperishable tear

Down the opening leaves of holy poets' pages.
   Thee not Orestes, not Electra mourns,
   But bending us-ward with memorial urns
The most high Muses that fulfil all ages
   Weep, and our God's heart yearns.

XIII

For, sparing of his sacred strength, not often
   Among us darkling here the lord of light
   Makes manifest his music and his might
In hearts that open and in lips that soften
   With the soft flame and heat of songs that shine.
   Thy lips indeed he touched with bitter wine,
And nourished them indeed with bitter bread,
   Yet surely from his hand thy soul's food came,
   The fire that scarred thy spirit at his flame
Was lighted, and thine hungering heart he fed
   Who feeds our hearts with fame.

XIV

Therefore he too now at thy soul's sunsetting,
   God of all suns and songs, he too bends down
   To mix his laurel with thy cypress crown,
And save thy dust from blame and from forgetting.
   Therefore he too, seeing all thou wert and art,
   Compassionate, with sad and sacred heart,
Mourns thee of many his children the last dead,
   And hallows with strange tears and alien sighs
   Thine unmelodious mouth and sunless eyes,
And over thine irrevocable head
   Sheds light from the under skies.

192

XV

And one weeps with him in the ways Lethean,
  And stains with tears her changing bosom chill,
  That obscure Venus of the hollow hill,
That thing transformed which was the Cytherean,
  With lips that lost their Grecian laugh divine
  Long since, and face no more called Erycine;
A ghost, a bitter and luxurious god.
  Thee also with fair flesh and singing spell
  Did she, a sad and second prey, compel
Into the footless places once more trod,
  And shadows hot from hell.

XVI

And now no sacred staff shall break in blossom,
  No choral salutation lure to light
  A spirit sick with perfume and sweet night
And love's tired eyes and hands and barren bosom.
  There is no help for these things; none to mend,
  And none to mar; not all our songs, O friend,
Will make death clear or make life durable.
  Howbeit with rose and ivy and wild vine
  And with wild notes about this dust of thine
At least I fill the place where white dreams dwell
  And wreathe an unseen shrine.

XVII

Sleep, and if life was bitter to thee, pardon,
  If sweet, give thanks, thou hast no more to live;
  And to give thanks is good, and to forgive.
Out of the mystic and the mournful garden

Where all day through thine hands in barren braid
  Wove the sick flowers of secrecy and shade,
Green buds of sorrow and sin, and remnants grey,
  Sweet-smelling, pale with poison, sanguine-hearted,
  Passions that sprang from sleep and thoughts that
                   started,
Shall death not bring us all as thee one day
  Among the days departed?

XVIII

For thee, O now a silent soul, my brother,
  Take at my hands this garland, and farewell.
  Thin is the leaf, and chill the wintry smell,
And chill the solemn earth, a fatal mother,
  With sadder than the Niobean womb,
  And in the hollow of her breasts a tomb.
Content thee, howsoe'er, whose days are done;
  There lies not any troublous thing before,
  Nor sight nor sound to war against thee more,
For whom all winds are quiet as the sun
  All waters as the shore.

ATALANTA IN CALYDON

The Argument

ALTHAEA, daughter of Thestius and Eurythemis, queen of Calydon, being with child of Meleager her first-born son, dreamed that she brought forth a brand burning; and upon his birth came the three Fates and prophesied of him three things, namely these: that he should have great strength of his hands, and good fortune in this life, and that he should live no longer when the brand then in the fire were consumed: wherefore his mother plucked it forth and kept it by her. And the child being a man grown sailed with Jason after the fleece of gold, and won himself great praise of all men living; and when the tribes of the north and west made war upon Aetolia, he fought against their army and scattered it. But Artemis, having at the first stirred up these tribes to war against Oeneus king of Calydon, because he had offered sacrifice to all the gods saving her alone, but her he had forgotten to honour, was yet more wroth because of the destruction of this army, and sent upon the land of Calydon a wild boar which slew many and wasted all their increase, but him could none slay, and many went against him and perished. Then were all the chief men of Greece gathered together, and among them Atalanta daughter of Iasius the Arcadian, a virgin; for whose sake Artemis let slay the boar, seeing she favoured the maiden greatly; and Meleager having despatched it gave the spoil thereof to Atalanta, as one beyond measure enamoured of her; but the brethren of Althaea his mother, Toxeus and Plexippus, with such others as misliked that she only should bear off the praise whereas many had borne the labour, laid wait for her to take away her spoil; but Meleager fought against them and slew them: whom when Althaea their sister beheld and knew to be slain of her son, she waxed for wrath and sorrow like as one mad, and taking the brand whereby the measure of her son's life was meted to him, she cast it upon a fire; and with the wasting thereof his life likewise wasted away, that being brought back to his father's house he died in a brief space; and his mother also endured not long after for very sorrow; and this was his end, and the end of that hunting.

The Persons

Chief Huntsman	Atalanta
Chorus	Toxeus
Althaea	Plexippus
Meleager	Herald
Oeneus	Messenger

Second Messenger

CHIEF HUNTSMAN

Maiden, and mistress of the months and stars
Now folded in the flowerless fields of heaven,
Goddess whom all gods love with threefold heart,
Being treble in thy divided deity,
A light for dead men and dark hours, a foot
Swift on the hills as morning, and a hand
To all things fierce and fleet that roar and range
Mortal, with gentler shafts than snow or sleep;
Hear now and help and lift no violent hand,
But favourable and fair as thine eye's beam
Hidden and shown in heaven; for I all night
Amid the king's hounds and the hunting men
Have wrought and worshipped toward thee; nor shall man
See goodlier hounds or deadlier edge of spears;
But for the end, that lies unreached at yet
Between the hands and on the knees of gods.
O fair-faced sun, killing the stars and dews
And dreams and desolation of the night!
Rise up, shine, stretch thine hand out, with thy bow
Touch the most dimmest height of trembling heaven,
And burn and break the dark about thy ways,
Shot through and through with arrows; let thine hair
Lighten as flame above that flameless shell
Which was the moon, and thine eyes fill the world
And thy lips kindle with swift beams; let earth
Laugh, and the long sea fiery from thy feet
Through all the roar and ripple of streaming springs
And foam in reddening flakes and flying flowers
Shaken from hands and blown from lips of nymphs
Whose hair or breast divides the wandering wave
With salt close tresses cleaving lock to lock,

All gold, or shuddering and unfurrowed snow;
And all the winds about thee with their wings,
And fountain-heads of all the watered world;
Each horn of Achelous, and the green
Euenus, wedded with the straitening sea.
For in fair time thou comest; come also thou,
Twin-born with him, and virgin, Artemis,
And give our spears their spoil, the wild boar's hide,
Sent in thine anger against us for sin done
And bloodless altars without wine or fire.
Him now consume thou; for thy sacrifice
With sanguine-shining steam divides the dawn,
And one, the maiden rose of all thy maids,
Arcadian Atalanta, snowy-souled,
Fair as the snow and footed as the wind,
From Ladon and well-wooded Maenalus
Over the firm hills and the fleeting sea
Hast thou drawn hither, and many an armèd king,
Heroes, the crown of men, like gods in fight.
Moreover out of all the Aetolian land,
From the full-flowered Lelantian pasturage
To what of fruitful field the son of Zeus
Won from the roaring river and labouring sea
When the wild god shrank in his horn and fled
And foamed and lessened through his wrathful fords
Leaving clear lands that steamed with sudden sun,
These virgins with the lightening of the day
Bring thee fresh wreaths and their own sweeter hair,
Luxurious locks and flower-like mixed with flowers,
Clean offering, and chaste hymns; but me the time
Divides from these things; whom do thou not less
Help and give honour, and to mine hounds good speed,
And edge to spears, and luck to each man's hand.

CHORUS

When the hounds of spring are on winter's traces,
   The mother of months in meadow or plain
Fills the shadows and windy places
   With lisp of leaves and ripple of rain;
And the brown bright nightingale amorous
Is half assuaged for Itylus,
For the Thracian ships and the foreign faces,
   The tongueless vigil, and all the pain.

Come with bows bent and with emptying of quivers,
   Maiden most perfect, lady of light,
With a noise of winds and many rivers,
   With a clamour of waters, and with might;
Bind on thy sandals, O thou most fleet,
Over the splendour and speed of thy feet;
For the faint east quickens, the wan west shivers,
   Round the feet of the day and the feet of the night.

Where shall we find her, how shall we sing to her,
   Fold our hands round her knees, and cling?
O that man's heart were as fire and could spring to her,
   Fire, or the strength of the streams that spring!
For the stars and the winds are unto her
As raiment, as songs of the harp-player;
For the risen stars and the fallen cling to her,
   And the south-west wind and the west wind sing.

For winter's rains and ruins are over,
   And all the season of snows and sins;
The days dividing lover and lover,
   The light that loses, the night that wins;

And time remembered is grief forgotten,
And frosts are slain and flowers begotten,
And in green underwood and cover
   Blossom by blossom the spring begins.

The full streams feed on flower of rushes,
   Ripe grasses trammel a travelling foot,
The faint fresh flame of the young year flushes
   From leaf to flower and flower to fruit;
And fruit and leaf are as gold and fire,
And the oat is heard above the lyre,
And the hoofèd heel of a satyr crushes
   The chestnut-husk at the chestnut-root.

And Pan by noon and Bacchus by night,
   Fleeter of foot than the fleet-foot kid,
Follows with dancing and fills with delight
   The Maenad and the Bassarid;
And soft as lips that laugh and hide
The laughing leaves of the trees divide,
And screen from seeing and leave in sight
   The god pursuing, the maiden hid.

The ivy falls with the Bacchanal's hair
   Over her eyebrows hiding her eyes;
The wild vine slipping down leaves bare
   Her bright breast shortening into sighs;
The wild vine slips with the weight of its leaves
But the berried ivy catches and cleaves
To the limbs that glitter, the feet that scare
   The wolf that follows, the fawn that flies.

ALTHAEA

What do ye singing? what is this ye sing?

CHORUS

Flowers bring we, and pure lips that please the gods,
And raiment meet for service: lest the day
Turn sharp with all its honey in our lips.

ALTHAEA

Night, a black hound, follows the white fawn day,
Swifter than dreams the white flown feet of sleep;
Will ye pray back the night with any prayers?
And though the spring put back a little while
Winter, and snows that plague all men for sin,
And the iron time of cursing, yet I know
Spring shall be ruined with the rain, and storm
Eat up like fire the ashen autumn days.
I marvel what men do with prayers awake
Who dream and die with dreaming; any god,
Yea the least god of all things called divine,
Is more than sleep and waking; yet we say,
Perchance by praying a man shall match his god.
For if sleep have no mercy, and man's dreams
Bite to the blood and burn into the bone,
What shall this man do waking? By the gods,
He shall not pray to dream sweet things tonight,
Having dreamt once more bitter things than death.

CHORUS

Queen, but what is it that hath burnt thine heart?
For thy speech flickers like a blown-out flame.

O   201

ALTHAEA

Look, ye say well, and know not what ye say;
For all my sleep is turned into a fire,
And all my dreams to stuff that kindles it.

CHORUS

Yet one doth well being patient of the gods.

ALTHAEA

Yea, lest they smite us with some four-foot plague.

CHORUS

But when time spreads find out some herb for it.

ALTHAEA

And with their healing herbs infect our blood.

CHORUS

What ails thee to be jealous of their ways?

ALTHAEA

What if they give us poisonous drinks for wine?

CHORUS

They have their will; much talking mends it not.

ALTHAEA

And gall for milk, and cursing for a prayer?

CHORUS

Have they not given life, and the end of life?

ALTHAEA

Lo, where they heal, they help not; thus they do,
They mock us with a little piteousness,
And we say prayers, and weep; but at the last,
Sparing awhile, they smite and spare no whit.

CHORUS

Small praise man gets dispraising the high gods:
What have they done that thou dishonourest them?

ALTHAEA

First Artemis for all this harried land
I praise not, and for wasting of the boar
That mars with tooth and tusk and fiery feet
Green pasturage and the grace of standing corn
And meadow and marsh with springs and unblown
                                             leaves,
Flocks and swift herds and all that bite sweet grass,
I praise her not; what things are these to praise?

CHORUS

But when the king did sacrifice, and gave
Each god fair dues of wheat and blood and wine,
Her not with bloodshed nor burnt-offering
Revered he, nor with salt or cloven cake;
Wherefore being wroth she plagued the land; but now
Takes off from us fate and her heavy things.
Which deed of these twain were not good to praise?
For a just deed looks always either way
With blameless eyes, and mercy is no fault.

ALTHAEA

Yea, but a curse she hath sent above all these
To hurt us where she healed us; and hath lit
Fire where the old fire went out, and where the wind
Slackened, hath blown on us with deadlier air.

CHORUS

What storm is this that tightens all our sail?

ALTHAEA

Love, a thwart sea-wind full of rain and foam.

CHORUS

Whence blown, and born under what stormier star?

ALTHAEA

Southward across Euenus from the sea.

CHORUS

Thy speech turns toward Arcadia like blown wind.

ALTHAEA

Sharp as the north sets when the snows are out.

CHORUS

Nay, for this maiden hath no touch of love.

ALTHAEA

I would she had sought in some cold gulf of sea
Love, or in dens where strange beasts lurk, or fire,
Or snows on the extreme hills, or iron land
Where no spring is; I would she had sought therein
And found, or ever love had found her here.

CHORUS

She is holier than all holy days or things,
The sprinkled water or fume of perfect fire;
Chaste, dedicated to pure prayers, and filled
With higher thoughts than heaven; a maiden clean,
Pure iron, fashioned for a sword; and man
She loves not; what should one such do with love?

ALTHAEA

Look you, I speak not as one light of wit,
But as a queen speaks, being heart-vexed; for oft
I hear my brothers wrangling in mid hall,
And am not moved; and my son chiding them,
And these things nowise move me, but I know
Foolish and wise men must be to the end,
And feed myself with patience; but this most,
This moves me, that for wise men as for fools
Love is one thing, an evil thing, and turns
Choice words and wisdom into fire and air.
And in the end shall no joy come, but grief,
Sharp words and soul's division and fresh tears
Flower-wise upon the old root of tears brought forth,
Fruit-wise upon the old flower of tears sprung up,
Pitiful sighs, and much regrafted pain.
These things are in my presage, and myself
Am part of them and know not; but in dreams
The gods are heavy on me, and all the fates
Shed fire across my eyelids mixed with night,
And burn me blind, and disilluminate
My sense of seeing, and my perspicuous soul
Darken with vision; seeing I see not, hear
And hearing am not holpen, but mine eyes

Stain many tender broideries in the bed
Drawn up about my face that I may weep
And the king wake not; and my brows and lips
Tremble and sob in sleeping, like swift flames
That tremble, or water when it sobs with heat
Kindled from under; and my tears fill my breast
And speck the fair dyed pillows round the king
With barren showers and salter than the sea,
Such dreams divide me dreaming; for long since
I dreamed that out of this my womb had sprung
Fire and a firebrand; this was ere my son,
Meleager, a goodly flower in fields of fight,
Felt the light touch him coming forth, and wailed
Childlike; but yet he was not; and in time
I bare him, and my heart was great; for yet
So royally was never strong man born,
Nor queen so nobly bore as noble a thing
As this my son was: such a birth God sent
And such a grace to bear it. Then came in
Three weaving women, and span each a thread,
Saying This for strength and That for luck, and one
Saying Till the brand upon the hearth burn down,
So long shall this man see good days and live.
And I with gathered raiment from the bed
Sprang, and drew forth the brand, and cast on it
Water, and trod the flame bare-foot, and crushed
With naked hand spark beaten out of spark
And blew against and quenched it; for I said,
These are the most high Fates that dwell with us,
And we find favour a little in their sight,
A little, and more we miss of, and much time
Foils us; howbeit they have pitied me, O son,
And thee most piteous, thee a tenderer thing

Than any flower of fleshly seed alive.
Wherefore I kissed and hid him with my hands,
And covered under arms and hair, and wept,
And feared to touch him with my tears, and laughed;
So light a thing was this man, grown so great
Men cast their heads back, seeing against the sun
Blaze the armed man carven on his shield, and hear
The laughter of little bells along the brace
Ring, as birds singing or flutes blown, and watch,
High up, the cloven shadow of either plume
Divide the bright light of the brass, and make
His helmet as a windy and wintering moon
Seen through blown cloud and plume-like drift, when
                                    ships
Drive, and men strive with all the sea, and oars
Break, and the beaks dip under, drinking death;
Yet was he then but a span long, and moaned
With inarticulate mouth inseparate words,
And with blind lips and fingers wrung my breast
Hard, and thrust out with foolish hands and feet,
Murmuring; but those grey women with bound hair
Who fright the gods frighted not him; he laughed
Seeing them, and pushed out hands to feel and haul
Distaff and thread, intangible; but they
Passed, and I hid the brand, and in my heart
Laughed likewise, having all my will of heaven.
But now I know not if to left or right
The gods have drawn us hither; for again
I dreamt, and saw the black brand burst on fire
As a branch bursts in flower, and saw the flame
Fade flower-wise, and Death came and with dry lips
Blew the charred ash into my breast; and Love
Trampled the ember and crushed it with swift feet.

This I have also at heart; that not for me,
Not for me only or son of mine, O girls,
The gods have wrought life, and desire of life,
Heart's love and heart's division; but for all
There shines one sun and one wind blows till night.
And when night comes the wind sinks and the sun,
And there is no light after, and no storm,
But sleep and much forgetfulness of things.
In such wise I gat knowledge of the gods
Years hence, and heard high sayings of one most wise,
Eurythemis my mother, who beheld
With eyes alive and spake with lips of these
As one on earth disfleshed and disallied
From breath or blood corruptible; such gifts
Time gave her, and an equal soul to these
And equal face to all things; thus she said.
But whatsoever intolerable or glad
The swift hours weave and unweave, I go hence
Full of mine own soul, perfect of myself,
Toward mine and me sufficient; and what chance
The gods cast lots for and shake out on us,
That shall we take, and that much bear withal.
And now, before these gather to the hunt,
I will go arm my son and bring him forth,
Lest love or some man's anger work him harm.

CHORUS

Before the beginning of years
   There came to the making of man
Time, with a gift of tears;
   Grief, with a glass that ran;
Pleasure, with pain for leaven;
   Summer, with flowers that fell;

Remembrance fallen from heaven,
   And madness risen from hell;
Strength without hands to smite;
   Love that endures for a breath:
Night, the shadow of light,
   And life, the shadow of death.

And the high gods took in hand
   Fire, and the falling of tears,
And a measure of sliding sand
   From under the feet of the years;
And froth and drift of the sea;
   And dust of the labouring earth;
And bodies of things to be
   In the houses of death and of birth;
And wrought with weeping and laughter,
   And fashioned with loathing and love
With life before and after
   And death beneath and above,
For a day and a night and a morrow,
   That his strength might endure for a span
With travail and heavy sorrow,
   The holy spirit of man.

From the winds of the north and the south
   They gathered as unto strife;
They breathed upon his mouth,
   They filled his body with life;
Eyesight and speech they wrought
   For the veils of the soul therein,
A time for labour and thought,
   A time to serve and to sin;
They gave him light in his ways,

And love, and a space for delight,
And beauty and length of days,
　And night, and sleep in the night.
His speech is a burning fire;
　With his lips he travaileth;
In his heart is a blind desire,
　In his eyes foreknowledge of death;
He weaves, and is clothed with derision;
　Sows, and he shall not reap;
His life is a watch or a vision
　Between a sleep and a sleep.

MELEAGER

O sweet new heaven and air without a star,
Fair day, be fair and welcome, as to men
With deeds to do and praise to pluck from thee.
Come forth a child, born with clear sound and light,
With laughter and swift limbs and prosperous looks;
That this great hunt with heroes for the hounds
May leave thee memorable and us well sped.

ALTHAEA

Son, first I praise thy prayer, then bid thee speed;
But the gods hear men's hands before their lips,
And heed beyond all crying and sacrifice
Light of things done and noise of labouring men.
But thou, being armed and perfect for the deed,
Abide; for like rain-flakes in a wind they grow,
The men thy fellows, and the choice of the world,
Bound to root out the tuskèd plague, and leave
Thanks and safe days and peace in Calydon.

MELEAGER

For the whole city and all the low-lying land
Flames, and the soft air sounds with them that come;
The gods give all these fruit of all their works.

ALTHAEA

Set thine eye thither and fix thy spirit and say
Whom there thou knowest; for sharp mixed shadow and
                              wind
Blown up between the morning and the mist,
With steam of steeds and flash of bridle or wheel,
And fire, and parcels of the broken dawn,
And dust divided by hard light, and spears
That shine and shift as the edge of wild beasts' eyes,
Smite upon mine; so fiery their blind edge
Burns, and bright points break up and baffle day.

MELEAGER

The first, for many I know not, being far off,
Peleus the Larissaean, couched with whom
Sleeps the white sea-bred wife and silver-shod,
Fair as fled foam, a goddess; and their son
Most swift and splendid of men's children born,
Most like a god, full of the future fame.

ALTHAEA

Who are these shining like one sundered star?

MELEAGER

Thy sister's sons, a double flower of men.

ALTHAEA

O sweetest kin to me in all the world,
O twin-born blood of Leda, gracious heads
Like kindled lights in untempestuous heaven,
Fair flower-like stars on the iron foam of fight,
With what glad heart and kindliness of soul,
Even to the staining of both eyes with tears
And kindling of warm eyelids with desire,
A great way off I greet you, and rejoice
Seeing you so fair, and moulded like as gods.
Far off ye come, and least in years of these,
But lordliest, but worth love to look upon.

MELEAGER

Even such (for sailing hither I saw far hence,
And where Eurotas hollows his moist rock
Nigh Sparta with a strenuous-hearted stream)
Even such I saw their sisters; one swan-white,
The little Helen, and less fair than she
Fair Clytaemnestra, grave as pasturing fawns
Who feed and fear some arrow; but at whiles,
As one smitten with love or wrung with joy,
She laughs and lightens with her eyes, and then
Weeps; whereat Helen, having laughed, weeps too,
And the other chides her, and she being chid speaks
                                        nought,
But cheeks and lips and eyelids kisses her,
Laughing; so fare they, as in their bloomless bud
And full of unblown life, the blood of gods.

ALTHAEA

Sweet days befall them and good loves and lords,
And tender and temperate honours of the hearth,

Peace, and a perfect life and blameless bed.
But who shows next an eagle wrought in gold,
That flames and beats broad wings against the sun
And with void mouth gapes after emptier prey?

MELEAGER

Know by that sign the reign of Telamon
Between the fierce mouths of the encountering brine
On the strait reefs of twice-washed Salamis.

ALTHAEA

For like one great of hand he bears himself,
Vine-chapleted, with savours of the sea,
Glittering as wine and moving as a wave.
But who girt round there roughly follows him?

MELEAGER

Ancaeus, great of hand, an iron bulk,
Two-edged for fight as the axe against his arm,
Who drives against the surge of stormy spears
Full-sailed; him Cepheus follows, his twin-born,
Chief name next his of all Arcadian men.

ALTHAEA

Praise be with men abroad; chaste lives with us,
Home-keeping days and household reverences.

MELEAGER

Next by the left unsandalled foot know thou
The sail and oar of this Aetolian land,
Thy brethren, Toxeus and the violent-souled
Plexippus, over-swift with hand and tongue;
For hands are fruitful, but the ignorant mouth
Blows and corrupts their work with barren breath.

ALTHAEA

Speech too bears fruit, being worthy; and air blows down
Things poisonous, and high-seated violences,
And with charmed words and songs have men put out
Wild evil, and the fire of tyrannies.

MELEAGER

Yea, all things have they, save the gods and love.

ALTHAEA

Love thou the law and cleave to things ordained.

MELEAGER

Law lives upon their lips whom these applaud.

ALTHAEA

How sayest thou these? what god applauds new things?

MELEAGER

Zeus, who hath fear and custom under foot.

ALTHAEA

But loves not laws thrown down and lives awry.

MELEAGER

Yet is not less himself than his own law.

ALTHAEA

Nor shifts and shuffles old things up and down.

MELEAGER

But what he will remoulds and discreates.

ALTHAEA

Much, but not this, that each thing live its life.

MELEAGER

Nor only live, but lighten and lift up higher.

ALTHAEA

Pride breaks itself, and too much gained is gone.

MELEAGER

Things gained are gone, but great things done endure.

ALTHAEA

Child, if a man serve law through all his life
And with his whole heart worship, him all gods
Praise; but who loves it only with his lips,
And not in heart and deed desiring it
Hides a perverse will with obsequious words,
Him heaven infatuates and his twin-born fate
Tracks, and gains on him, scenting sins far off,
And the swift hounds of violent death devour.
Be man at one with equal-minded gods,
So shall he prosper; not through laws torn up,
Violated rule and a new face of things.
A woman armed makes war upon herself,
Unwomanlike, and treads down use and wont
And the sweet common honour that she hath,
Love, and the cry of children, and the hand
Trothplight and mutual mouth of marriages,
This doth she, being unloved; whom if one love,
Not fire nor iron and the wide-mouthed wars
Are deadlier than her lips or braided hair.

For of the one comes poison, and a curse
Falls from the other and burns the lives of men.
But thou, son, be not filled with evil dreams,
Nor with desire of these things; for with time
Blind love burns out; but if one feed it full
Till some discolouring stain dyes all his life,
He shall keep nothing praiseworthy, nor die
The sweet wise death of old men honourable,
Who have lived out all the length of all their years
Blameless, and seen well-pleased the face of gods,
And without shame and without fear have wrought
Things memorable, and while their days held out
In sight of all men and the sun's great light
Have gat them glory and given of their own praise
To the earth that bare them and the day that bred,
Home friends and far-off hospitalities,
And filled with gracious and memorial fame
Lands loved of summer or washed by violent seas,
Towns populous and many unfooted ways,
And alien lips and native with their own.
But when white age and venerable death
Mow down the strength and life within their limbs,
Drain out the blood and darken their clear eyes,
Immortal honour is on them, having past
Through splendid life and death desirable
To the clear seat and remote throne of souls,
Lands indiscoverable in the unheard-of west,
Round which the strong stream of a sacred sea
Rolls without wind for ever, and the snow
There shows not her white wings and windy feet,
Nor thunder nor swift rain saith anything,
Nor the sun burns, but all things rest and thrive;
And these, filled full of days, divine and dead,

Sages and singers fiery from the god,
And such as loved their land and all things good
And, best beloved of best men, liberty,
Free lives and lips, free hands of men free-born,
And whatsoever on earth was honourable
And whosoever of all the ephemeral seed,
Live there a life no liker to the gods
But nearer than their life of terrene days.
Love thou such life and look for such a death.
But from the light and fiery dreams of love
Spring heavy sorrows and a sleepless life,
Visions not dreams, whose lids no charm shall close
Nor song assuage them waking; and swift death
Crushes with sterile feet the unripening ear,
Treads out the timeless vintage; whom do thou
Eschewing embrace the luck of this thy life,
Not without honour; and it shall bear to thee
Such fruit as men reap from spent hours and wear,
Few men, but happy; of whom be thou, O son,
Happiest, if thou submit thy soul to fate,
And set thine eyes and heart on hopes high-born
And divine deeds and abstinence divine.
So shalt thou be toward all men all thy days
As light and might communicable, and burn
From heaven among the stars above the hours,
And break not as a man breaks nor burn down:
For to whom other of all heroic names
Have the gods given his life in hand as thine?
And gloriously hast thou lived, and made thy life
To me that bare thee and to all men born
Thankworthy, a praise for ever; and hast won fame
When wild wars broke all round thy father's house,
And the mad people of windy mountain ways

Laid spears against us like a sea, and all
Aetolia thundered with Thessalian hoofs;
Yet these, as wind baffles the foam, and beats
Straight back the relaxed ripple, didst thou break
And loosen all their lances, till undone
And man from man they fell; for ye twain stood
God against god, Ares and Artemis,
And thou the mightier; wherefore she unleashed
A sharp-toothed curse thou too shalt overcome;
For in the greener blossom of thy life
Ere the full blade caught flower, and when time gave
Respite, thou didst not slacken soul nor sleep,
But with great hand and heart seek praise of men
Out of sharp straits and many a grievous thing,
Seeing the strange foam of undivided seas
On channels never sailed in, and by shores
Where the old winds cease not blowing, and all the night
Thunders, and day is no delight to men.

CHORUS

Meleager, a noble wisdom and fair words
The gods have given this woman; hear thou these.

MELEAGER

O mother, I am not fain to strive in speech
Nor set my mouth against thee, who art wise
Even as they say and full of sacred words.
But one thing I know surely, and cleave to this;
That though I be not subtle of wit as thou
Nor womanlike to weave sweet words, and melt
Mutable minds of wise men as with fire,
I too, doing justly and reverencing the gods,
Shall not want wit to see what things be right.

For whom they love and whom reject, being gods,
There is no man but seeth, and in good time
Submits himself, refraining all his heart.
And I too as thou sayest have seen great things;
Seen otherwhere, but chiefly when the sail
First caught between stretched ropes the roaring west,
And all our oars smote eastward, and the wind
First flung round faces of seafaring men
White splendid snow-flakes of the sundering foam,
And the first furrow in virginal green sea
Followed the plunging ploughshare of hewn pine,
And closed, as when deep sleep subdues man's breath
Lips close and heart subsides; and closing, shone
Sunlike with many a Nereid's hair, and moved
Round many a trembling mouth of doubtful gods,
Risen out of sunless and sonorous gulfs
Through waning water and into shallow light,
That watched us; and when flying the dove was snared
As with men's hands, but we shot after and sped
Clear through the irremeable Symplegades;
And chiefliest when hoar beach and herbless cliff
Stood out ahead from Colchis, and we heard
Clefts hoarse with wind, and saw through narrowing reefs
The lightning of the intolerable wave
Flash, and the white wet flame of breakers burn
Far under a kindling south wind, as a lamp
Burns and bends all its blowing flame one way;
Wild heights untravelled of the wind, and vales
Cloven seaward by their violent streams, and white
With bitter flowers and bright salt scurf of brine;
Heard sweep their sharp swift gales, and bowing birdwise
Shriek with birds' voices, and with furious feet
Tread loose the long skirts of a storm; and saw

The whole white Euxine clash together and fall
Full-mouthed, and thunderous from a thousand throats:
Yet we drew thither and won the fleece and won
Medea, deadlier than the sea; but there
Seeing many a wonder and fearful things to men
I saw not one thing like this one seen here,
Most fair and fearful, feminine, a god,
Faultless; whom I that love not, being unlike,
Fear, and give honour, and choose from all the gods.

OENEUS

Lady, the daughter of Thestius, and thou, son,
Not ignorant of your strife nor light of wit,
Scared with vain dreams and fluttering like spent fire,
I come to judge between you, but a king
Full of past days and wise from years endured.
Nor thee I praise, who art fain to undo things done:
Nor thee, who art swift to esteem them overmuch.
For what the hours have given is given, and this
Changeless; howbeit these change, and in good time
Devise new things and good, not one thing still.
Us have they sent now at our need for help
Among men armed a woman, foreign born,
Virgin, not like the natural flower of things
That grows and bears and brings forth fruit and dies;
Unlovable, no light for a husband's house,
Espoused; a glory among unwedded girls,
And chosen of gods who reverence maidenhood.
These too we honour in honouring her; but thou,
Abstain thy feet from following, and thine eyes
From amorous touch; nor set towards her thine heart,
Son, lest hate bear no deadlier fruit than love.

ALTHAEA

O king, thou art wise, but wisdom halts; and just,
But the gods love not justice more than fate,
And smite the righteous and the violent mouth,
And mix with insolent blood the reverent man's,
And bruise the holier as the lying lips.
Enough; for wise words fail me, and my heart
Takes fire and trembles flamewise, O my son,
O child, for thine head's sake; mine eyes wax thick,
Turning toward thee, so goodly a weaponed man,
So glorious; and for love of thine own eyes
They are darkened, and tears burn them, fierce as fire,
And my lips pause and my soul sinks with love.
But by thine hand, by thy sweet life and eyes,
By thy great heart and these clasped knees, O son,
I pray thee that thou slay me not with thee.
For there was never a mother woman-born
Loved her sons better; and never a queen of men
More perfect in her heart toward whom she loved.
For what lies light on many and they forget,
Small things and transitory as a wind o' the sea,
I forget never; I have seen thee all thine years
A man in arms, strong and a joy to men
Seeing thine head glitter and thine hand burn its way
Through a heavy and iron furrow of sundering spears;
But always also a flower of three suns old,
The small one thing that lying drew down my life
To lie with thee and feed thee; a child and weak,
Mine, a delight to no man, sweet to me.
Who then sought to thee? who gat help? who knew
If thou wert goodly? nay, no man at all.
Or what sea saw thee, or sounded with thine oar,

Child? or what strange land shone with war through
                                        thee?
But fair for me thou wert, O little life,
Fruitless, the fruit of mine own flesh, and blind,
More than much gold, ungrown, a foolish flower.
For silver nor bright snow nor feather of foam
Was whiter, and no gold yellower than thine hair,
O child, my child; and now thou art lordlier grown,
Not lovelier, nor a new thing in mine eyes,
I charge thee by thy soul and this my breast,
Fear thou the gods and me and thine own heart,
Lest all these turn against thee; for who knows
What wind upon what wave of altering time
Shall speak a storm and blow calamity?
And there is nothing stabile in the world
But the gods break it; yet not less, fair son,
If but one thing be stronger, if one endure,
Surely the bitter and the rooted love
That burns between us, going from me to thee,
Shall more endure than all things. What dost thou,
Following strange loves? why wilt thou kill mine heart?
Lo, I talk wild and windy words, and fall
From my clear wits, and seem of mine own self
Dethroned, dispraised, disseated; and my mind,
That was my crown, breaks, and mine heart is gone,
And I am naked of my soul, and stand
Ashamed, as a mean woman; take thou thought:
Live if thou wilt, and if thou wilt not, look,
The gods have given thee life to lose or keep,
Thou shalt not die as men die, but thine end
Fallen upon thee shall break me unaware.

MELEAGER

Queen, my whole heart is molten with thy tears,
And my limbs yearn with pity of thee, and love
Compels with grief mine eyes and labouring breath;
For what thou art I know thee, and this thy breast
And thy fair eyes I worship, and am bound
Toward thee in spirit and love thee in all my soul.
For there is nothing terribler to men
Than the sweet face of mothers, and the might.
But what shall be let be; for us the day
Once only lives a little, and is not found.
Time and the fruitful hour are more than we,
And these lay hold upon us; but thou, God,
Zeus, the sole steersman of the helm of things,
Father, be swift to see us, and as thou wilt
Help: or if adverse, as thou wilt, refrain.

CHORUS

We have seen thee, O Love, thou art fair; thou art
　　　　　　goodly, O Love;
Thy wings make light in the air as the wings of a dove.
Thy feet are as winds that divide the stream of the sea;
Earth is thy covering to hide thee, the garment of thee.
Thou art swift and subtle and blind as a flame of fire;
Before thee the laughter, behind thee the tears of desire;
And twain go forth beside thee, a man with a maid;
Her eyes are the eyes of a bride whom delight makes afraid;
As the breath in the buds that stir is her bridal breath:
But Fate is the name of her; and his name is Death.

For an evil blossom was born
　　Of sea-foam and the frothing of blood,

Blood-red and bitter of fruit,
   And the seed of it laughter and tears,
And the leaves of it madness and scorn;
  A bitter flower from the bud,
    Sprung of the sea without root,
      Sprung without graft from the years.

The weft of the world was untorn
  That is woven of the day on the night,
  The hair of the hours was not white
Nor the raiment of time overworn,
  When a wonder, a world's delight,
A perilous goddess was born;
  And the waves of the sea as she came
Clove, and the foam at her feet,
    Fawning, rejoiced to bring forth
  A fleshly blossom, a flame
Filling the heavens with heat
    To the cold white ends of the north.

And in air the clamorous birds,
  And men upon earth that hear
Sweet articulate words
    Sweetly divided apart,
  And in shallow and channel and mere
The rapid and footless herds,
    Rejoiced, being foolish of heart.

For all they said upon earth,
  She is fair, she is white like a dove,
    And the life of the world in her breath
Breathes, and is born at her birth;

For they knew thee for mother of love,
   And knew thee not mother of death.

What hadst thou to do being born,
   Mother, when winds were at ease,
As a flower of the springtime of corn,
   A flower of the foam of the seas?
For bitter thou wast from thy birth,
   Aphrodite, a mother of strife;
For before thee some rest was on earth,
   A little respite from tears,
   A little pleasure of life;
For life was not then as thou art,
   But as one that waxeth in years
Sweet-spoken, a fruitful wife;
   Earth had no thorn, and desire
No sting, neither death any dart;
   What hadst thou to do amongst these,
   Thou, clothed with a burning fire,
Thou, girt with sorrow of heart,
   Thou, sprung of the seed of the seas
As an ear from a seed of corn,
   As a brand plucked forth of a pyre,
As a ray shed forth of the morn,
   For division of soul and disease,
For a dart and a sting and a thorn?
What ailed thee then to be born?

Was there not evil enough,
   Mother, and anguish on earth
   Born with a man at his birth,
Wastes underfoot, and above
   Storm out of heaven and dearth

Shaken down from the shining thereof,
   Wrecks from afar overseas
And peril of shallow and firth,
   And tears that spring and increase
In the barren places of mirth,
That thou, having wings as a dove,
   Being girt with desire for a girth,
   That thou must come after these,
That thou must lay on him love?

Thou shouldst not so have been born:
   But death should have risen with thee,
   Mother, and visible fear,
     Grief, and the wringing of hands,
And noise of many that mourn;
   The smitten bosom, the knee
     Bowed, and in each man's ear
     A cry as of perishing lands,
A moan as of people in prison,
   A tumult of infinite griefs;
     And thunder of storm on the sands,
     And wailing of wives on the shore;
And under thee newly arisen
   Loud shoals and shipwrecking reefs,
     Fierce air and violent light;
     Sail rent and sundering oar,
     Darkness, and noises of night;
Clashing of streams in the sea,
   Wave against wave as a sword,
     Clamour of currents, and foam;
     Rains making ruin on earth,
     Winds that wax ravenous and roam
As wolves in a wolfish horde;

Fruits growing faint in the tree,
    And blind things dead in their birth;
  Famine, and blighting of corn,
  When thy time was come to be born.

All these we know of; but thee
  Who shall discern or declare?
In the uttermost ends of the sea
  The light of thine eyelids and hair,
    The light of thy bosom as fire
      Between the wheel of the sun
  And the flying flames of the air?
    Wilt thou turn thee not yet nor have pity,
But abide with despair and desire
  And the crying of armies undone,
    Lamentation of one with another
    And breaking of city by city;
  The dividing of friend against friend,
    The severing of brother and brother;
  Wilt thou utterly bring to an end?
  Have mercy, mother!

For against all men from of old
  Thou hast set thine hand as a curse,
  And cast out gods from their places.
    These things are spoken of thee.
Strong kings and goodly with gold
  Thou hast found out arrows to pierce,
    And made their kingdoms and races
    As dust and surf of the sea.
All these, overburdened with woes
  And with length of their days waxen weak,
    Thou slewest; and sentest moreover
    Upon Tyro an evil thing,

Rent hair and a fetter and blows
   Making bloody the flower of the cheek,
     Though she lay by a god as a lover,
       Though fair, and the seed of a king.
For of old, being full of thy fire,
   She endured not longer to wear
     On her bosom a saffron vest,
       On her shoulder an ashwood quiver;
Being mixed and made one through desire
   With Enipeus, and all her hair
     Made moist with his mouth, and her breast
       Filled full of the foam of the river.

ATALANTA

Sun, and clear light among green hills, and day
Late risen and long sought after, and you just gods
Whose hands divide anguish and recompense,
But first the sun's white sister, a maid in heaven,
On earth of all maids worshipped—hail, and hear,
And witness with me if not without sign sent,
Not without rule and reverence, I a maid
Hallowed, and huntress holy as whom I serve,
Here in your sight and eyeshot of these men
Stand, girt as they toward hunting, and my shafts
Drawn; wherefore all ye stand up on my side,
If I be pure and all ye righteous gods,
Lest one revile me, a woman, yet no wife,
That bear a spear for spindle, and this bow strung
For a web woven; and with pure lips salute
Heaven, and the face of all the gods, and dawn
Filling with maiden flames and maiden flowers
The starless fold o' the stars, and making sweet
The warm wan heights of the air, moon-trodden ways

And breathless gates and extreme hills of heaven.
Whom, having offered water and bloodless gifts,
Flowers, and a golden circlet of pure hair,
Next Artemis I bid be favourable
And make this day all golden, hers and ours,
Gracious and good and white to the unblamed end.
But thou, O well-beloved, of all my days
Bid it be fruitful, and a crown for all,
To bring forth leaves and bind round all my hair
With perfect chaplets woven for thine of thee.
For not without the word of thy chaste mouth,
For not without law given and clean command,
Across the white straits of the running sea
From Elis even to the Acheloian horn,
I with clear winds came hither and gentle gods,
Far off my father's house, and left uncheered
Iasius, and uncheered the Arcadian hills
And all their green-haired waters, and all woods
Disconsolate, to hear no horn of mine
Blown, and behold no flash of swift white feet.

MELEAGER

For thy name's sake and awe toward thy chaste head,
O holiest Atalanta, no man dares
Praise thee, though fairer than whom all men praise,
And godlike for thy grace of hallowed hair
And holy habit of thine eyes, and feet
That make the blown foam neither swift nor white
Though the wind winnow and whirl it; yet we praise
Gods, found because of thee adorable
And for thy sake praiseworthiest from all men:
Thee therefore we praise also, thee as these,
Pure, and a light lit at the hands of gods.

TOXEUS

How long will ye whet spears with eloquence,
Fight, and kill beasts dry-handed with sweet words?
Cease, or talk still and slay thy boars at home.

PLEXIPPUS

Why, if she ride among us for a man,
Sit thou for her and spin; a man grown girl
Is worth a woman weaponed; sit thou here.

MELEAGER

Peace, and be wise; no gods love idle speech.

PLEXIPPUS

Nor any man a man's mouth woman-tongued.

MELEAGER

For my lips bite not sharper than mine hands.

PLEXIPPUS

Nay, both bite soft, but no whit softly mine.

MELEAGER

Keep thine hands clean; they have time enough to stain.

PLEXIPPUS

For thine shall rest and wax not red today.

MELEAGER

Have all thy will of words; talk out thine heart.

ALTHAEA

Refrain your lips, O brethren, and my son,
Lest words turn snakes and bite you uttering them.

TOXEUS

Except she give her blood before the gods,
What profit shall a maid be among men?

PLEXIPPUS

Let her come crowned and stretch her throat for a knife,
Bleat out her spirit and die, and so shall men
Through her too prosper and through prosperous gods,
But nowise through her living; shall she live
A flower-bud of the flower-bed, or sweet fruit
For kisses and the honey-making mouth,
And play the shield for strong men and the spear?
Then shall the heifer and her mate lock horns,
And the bride overbear the groom, and men
Gods; for no less division sunders these;
Since all things made are seasonable in time,
But if one alter unseasonable are all.
But thou, O Zeus, hear me that I may slay
This beast before thee and no man halve with me
Nor woman, lest these mock thee, though a god,
Who hast made men strong, and thou being wise be held
Foolish; for wise is that thing which endures.

ATALANTA

Men, and the chosen of all this people, and thou,
King, I beseech you a little bear with me.
For if my life be shameful that I live,
Let the gods witness and their wrath; but these

Cast no such word against me. Thou, O mine,
O holy, O happy goddess, if I sin
Changing the words of women and the works
For spears and strange men's faces, hast not thou
One shaft of all thy sudden seven that pierced
Seven through the bosom or shining throat or side,
All couched about one mother's loosening knees,
All holy born, engraffed of Tantalus?
But if toward any of you I am overbold
That take thus much upon me, let him think
How I, for all my forest holiness,
Fame, and this armed and iron maidenhood,
Pay thus much also; I shall have no man's love
For ever, and no face of children born
Or feeding lips upon me or fastening eyes
For ever, nor being dead shall kings my sons
Mourn me and bury, and tears on daughters' cheeks
Burn; but a cold and sacred life, but strange,
But far from dances and the back-blowing torch,
Far off from flowers or any bed of man,
Shall my life be for ever: me the snows
That face the first o' the morning, and cold hills
Full of the land-wind and sea-travelling storms
And many a wandering wing of noisy nights
That know the thunder and hear the thickening wolves—
Me the utmost pine and footless frost of woods
That talk with many winds and gods, the hours
Re-risen, and white divisions of the dawn,
Springs thousand-tongued with the intermitting reed
And streams that murmur of the mother snow—
Me these allure, and know me; but no man
Knows, and my goddess only. Lo now, see
If one of all you these things vex at all.

Would God that any of you had all the praise
And I no manner of memory when I die,
So might I show before her perfect eyes
Pure, whom I follow, a maiden to my death.
But for the rest let all have all they will;
For is it a grief to you that I have part,
Being woman merely, in your male might and deeds
Done by main strength? yet in my body is throned
As great a heart, and in my spirit, O men,
I have not less of godlike. Evil it were
That one a coward should mix with you, one hand
Fearful, one eye abase itself; and these
Well might ye hate and well revile, not me.
For not the difference of the several flesh
Being vile or noble or beautiful or base
Makes praiseworthy, but purer spirit and heart
Higher than these meaner mouths and limbs, that feed,
Rise, rest, and are and are not; and for me,
What should I say? but by the gods of the world
And this my maiden body, by all oaths
That bind the tongue of men and the evil will,
I am not mighty-minded, nor desire
Crowns, nor the spoil of slain things nor the fame;
Feed ye on these, eat and wax fat; cry out,
Laugh, having eaten, and leap without a lyre,
Sing, mix the wind with clamour, smite and shake
Sonorous timbrels and tumultuous hair,
And fill the dance up with tempestuous feet,
For I will none; but having prayed my prayers
And made thank-offering for prosperities,
I shall go hence and no man see me more.
What thing is this for you to shout me down,
What, for a man to grudge me this my life

As it were envious of all yours, and I
A thief of reputations; nay, for now,
If there be any highest in heaven, a god
Above all thrones and thunders of the gods
Throned, and the wheel of the world roll under him,
Judge he between me and all of you, and see
If I transgress at all: but ye, refrain
Transgressing hands and reinless mouths, and keep
Silence, lest by much foam of violent words
And proper poison of your lips ye die.

OENEUS

O flower of Tegea, maiden, fleetest foot
And holiest head of women, have good cheer
Of thy good words: but ye, depart with her
In peace and reverence, each with blameless eye
Following his fate; exalt your hands and hearts,
Strike, cease not, arrow on arrow and wound on wound,
And go with gods and with the gods return.

CHORUS

Who hath given man speech? or who hath set therein
A thorn for peril and a snare for sin?
For in the word his life is and his breath,
    And in the word his death,
That madness and the infatuate heart may breed
    From the word's womb the deed
And life bring one thing forth ere all pass by,
Even one thing which is ours yet cannot die—
Death. Hast thou seen him ever anywhere,
Time's twin-born brother, imperishable as he
Is perishable and plaintive, clothed with care

And mutable as sand,
But death is strong and full of blood and fair
And perdurable and like a lord of land?
Nay, time thou seest not, death thou wilt not see
Till life's right hand be loosened from thine hand
   And thy life-days from thee.

For the gods very subtly fashion
   Madness with sadness upon earth:
Not knowing in any wise compassion,
   Nor holding pity of any worth;
And many things they have given and taken,
   And wrought and ruined many things;
The firm land have they loosed and shaken,
   And sealed the sea with all her springs;
They have wearied time with heavy burdens
   And vexed the lips of life with breath:
Set men to labour and given them guerdons,
   Death, and great darkness after death:
Put moans into the bridal measure
   And on the bridal wools a stain
And circled pain about with pleasure,
   And girdled pleasure about with pain;
And strewed one marriage-bed with tears and fire
For extreme loathing and supreme desire.

What shall be done with all these tears of ours?
   Shall they make watersprings in the fair heaven
To bathe the brows of morning? or like flowers
Be shed and shine before the starriest hours,
   Or made the raiment of the weeping Seven?
Or rather, O our masters, shall they be
Food for the famine of the grievous sea,

A great well-head of lamentation
Satiating the sad gods? or fall and flow
Among the years and seasons to and fro,
   And wash their feet with tribulation
And fill them full with grieving ere they go?
   Alas, our lords, and yet alas again,
Seeing all your iron heaven is gilt as gold
   But all we smite thereat in vain;
Smite the gates barred with groanings manifold,
   But all the floors are paven with our pain.
Yea, and with weariness of lips and eyes,
With breaking of the bosom, and with sighs,
   We labour, and are clad and fed with grief
And filled with days we would not fain behold
And nights we would not hear of; we wax old,
   All we wax old and wither like a leaf.
We are outcast, strayed between bright sun and moon;
   Our light and darkness are as leaves of flowers,
Black flowers and white, that perish; and the noon
   As midnight, and the night as daylight hours.
   A little fruit a little while is ours,
     And the worm finds it soon.

But up in heaven the high gods one by one
   Lay hands upon the draught that quickeneth,
Fulfilled with all tears shed and all things done,
   And stir with soft imperishable breath
   The bubbling bitterness of life and death,
And hold it to our lips and laugh; but they
Preserve their lips from tasting night or day,
   Lest they too change and sleep, the fates that spun,
The lips that made us and the hands that slay;
   Lest all these change, and heaven bow down to none,

236

Change and be subject to the secular sway
　　And terrene revolution of the sun.
Therefore they thrust it from them, putting time away.

I would the wine of time, made sharp and sweet
　　With multitudinous days and nights and tears
　　And many mixing savours of strange years,
Were no more trodden of them under feet,
　　Cast out and spilt about their holy places:
That life were given them as a fruit to eat
And death to drink as water; that the light
Might ebb, drawn backward from their eyes, and night
　　Hide for one hour the imperishable faces.
That they might rise up sad in heaven, and know
Sorrow and sleep, one paler than young snow,
　　One cold as blight of dew and ruinous rain;
Rise up and rest and suffer a little, and be
Awhile as all things born with us and we,
　　And grieve as men, and like slain men be slain.

For now we know not of them; but one saith
　　The gods are gracious, praising God; and one,
When hast thou seen? or hast thou felt his breath
　　Touch, nor consume thine eyelids as the sun,
Nor fill thee to the lips with fiery death?
　　None hath beheld him, none
Seen above other gods and shapes of things,
Swift without feet and flying without wings,
Intolerable, not clad with death or life,
　　Insatiable, not known of night or day,
The lord of love and loathing and of strife
　　Who gives a star and takes a sun away;
Who shapes the soul, and makes her a barren wife

To the earthly body and grievous growth of clay;
Who turns the large limbs to a little flame
And binds the great sea with a little sand;
Who makes desire, and slays desire with shame;
Who shakes the heaven as ashes in his hand;
Who, seeing the light and shadow for the same,
Bids day waste night as fire devours a brand,
Smites without sword, and scourges without rod;
The supreme evil, God.
Yea, with thine hate, O God, thou hast covered us,
One saith, and hidden our eyes away from sight,
And made us transitory and hazardous,
Light things and slight;
Yet have men praised thee, saying, He hath made man
thus,
And he doeth right.
Thou hast kissed us, and hast smitten; thou hast laid
Upon us with thy left hand life, and said,
Live: and again thou hast said, Yield up your breath,
And with thy right hand laid upon us death.
Thou hast sent us sleep, and stricken sleep with dreams,
Saying, Joy is not, but love of joy shall be;
Thou hast made sweet springs for all the pleasant streams,
In the end thou hast made them bitter with the sea.
Thou hast fed one rose with dust of many men;
Thou hast marred one face with fire of many tears;
Thou hast taken love, and given us sorrow again;
With pain thou hast filled us full to the eyes and ears.
Therefore because thou art strong, our father, and we
Feeble; and thou art against us, and thine hand
Constrains us in the shallows of the sea
And breaks us at the limits of the land;
Because thou hast bent thy lightnings as a bow,

And loosed the hours like arrows; and let fall
Sins and wild words and many a wingèd woe
    And wars among us, and one end of all;
Because thou hast made the thunder, and thy feet
    Are as a rushing water when the skies
Break, but thy face as an exceeding heat
    And flames of fire the eyelids of thine eyes;
Because thou art over all who are over us;
    Because thy name is life and our name death;
Because thou art cruel and men are piteous,
    And our hands labour and thine hand scattereth;
Lo, with hearts rent and knees made tremulous,
    Lo, with ephemeral lips and casual breath,
        At least we witness of thee ere we die
That these things are not otherwise, but thus;
    That each man in his heart sigheth, and saith,
        That all men even as I,
All we are against thee, against thee, O God most high.

    But ye, keep ye on earth
    Your lips from over-speech,
Loud words and longing are so little worth;
    And the end is hard to reach.
For silence after grievous things is good,
    And reverence, and the fear that makes men whole,
And shame, and righteous governance of blood,
    And lordship of the soul.
But from sharp words and wits men pluck no fruit,
And gathering thorns they shake the tree at root;
For words divide and rend;
But silence is most noble till the end.

ALTHAEA

I heard within the house a cry of news

And came forth eastward hither, where the dawn
Cheers first these warder gods that face the sun
And next our eyes unrisen; for unaware
Came clashes of swift hoofs and trampling feet
And through the windy pillared corridor
Light sharper than the frequent flames of day
That daily fill it from the fiery dawn;
Gleams, and a thunder of people that cried out,
And dust and hurrying horsemen; lo their chief,
That rode with Oeneus rein by rein, returned.
What cheer, O herald of my lord the king?

HERALD

Lady, good cheer and great; the boar is slain.

CHORUS

Praised be all gods that look towards Calydon.

ALTHAEA

Good news and brief; but by whose happier hand?

HERALD

A maiden's and a prophet's and thy son's.

ALTHAEA

Well fare the spear that severed him and life.

HERALD

Thine own, and not an alien, hast thou blest.

ALTHAEA

Twice be thou too for my sake blest and his.

HERALD

At the king's word I rode afoam for thine.

ALTHAEA

Thou sayest he tarrieth till they bring the spoil?

HERALD

Hard by the quarry, where they breathe, O queen.

ALTHAEA

Speak thou their chance; but some bring flowers and
                             crown
These gods and all the lintel, and shed wine,
Fetch sacrifice and slay; for heaven is good.

HERALD

Some furlongs northward where the brakes begin
West of that narrowing range of warrior hills
Whose brooks have bled with battle when thy son
Smote Acarnania, there all they made halt,
And with keen eye took note of spear and hound,
Royally ranked; Laertes island-born,
The young Gerenian Nestor, Panopeus,
And Cepheus and Ancaeus, mightiest thewed,
Arcadians; next, and evil-eyed of these,
Arcadian Atalanta, with twain hounds
Lengthening the leash, and under nose and brow
Glittering with lipless tooth and fire-swift eye;
But from her white braced shoulder the plumed shafts
Rang, and the bow shone from her side; next her
Meleager, like a sun in spring that strikes
Branch into leaf and bloom into the world,

241

A glory among men meaner; Iphicles,
And following him that slew the biform bull
Pirithous, and divine Eurytion,
And, bride-bound to the gods, Aeacides.
Then Telamon his brother, and Argive-born
The seer and sayer of visions and of truth,
Amphiaraus; and a four-fold strength,
Thine, even thy mother's and thy sister's sons.
And recent from the roar of foreign foam
Jason, and Dryas twin-begot with war,
A blossom of bright battle, sword and man
Shining; and Idas, and the keenest eye
Of Lynceus, and Admetus twice-espoused,
And Hippasus and Hyleus, great in heart.
These having halted bade blow horns, and rode
Through woods and waste lands cleft by stormy streams,
Past yew-trees and the heavy hair of pines,
And where the dew is thickest under oaks,
This way and that; but questing up and down
They saw no trail nor scented; and one said,
Plexippus, Help, or help not, Artemis,
And we will flay thy boarskin with male hands;
But saying, he ceased and said not that he would,
Seeing where the green ooze of a sun-struck marsh
Shook with a thousand reeds untunable,
And in their moist and multitudinous flower
Slept no soft sleep, with violent visions fed,
The blind bulk of the immeasurable beast.
And seeing, he shuddered with sharp lust of praise
Through all his limbs, and launched a double dart.
And missed; for much desire divided him,
Too hot of spirit and feebler than his will,
That his hand failed, though fervent; and the shaft,

Sundering the rushes, in a tamarisk stem
Shook, and stuck fast; then all abode save one,
The Arcadian Atalanta; from her side
Sprang her hounds, labouring at the leash, and slipped,
And plashed ear-deep with plunging feet; but she
Saying, Speed it as I send it for thy sake,
Goddess, drew bow and loosed; the sudden string
Rang, and sprang inward, and the waterish air
Hissed, and the moist plumes of the songless reeds
Moved as a wave which the wind moves no more.
But the boar heaved half out of ooze and slime
His tense flank trembling round the barbèd wound,
Hateful; and fiery with invasive eyes
And bristling with intolerable hair
Plunged, and the hounds clung, and green flowers and
white
Reddened and broke all round them where they came.
And charging with sheer tusk he drove, and smote
Hyleus; and sharp death caught his sudden soul,
And violent sleep shed night upon his eyes.
Then Peleus, with strong strain of hand and heart,
Shot; but the sidelong arrow slid, and slew
His comrade born and loving countryman,
Under the left arm smitten, as he no less
Poised a like arrow; and bright blood brake afoam,
And falling, and weighed back by clamorous arms,
Sharp rang the dead limbs of Eurytion.
Then one shot happier, the Cadmean seer,
Amphiaraus; for his sacred shaft
Pierced the red circlet of one ravening eye
Beneath the brute brows of the sanguine boar,
Now bloodier from one slain; but he so galled
Sprang straight, and rearing cried no lesser cry

Than thunder and the roar of wintering streams
That mix their own foam with the yellower sea;
And as a tower that falls by fire in fight
With ruin of walls and all its archery,
And breaks the iron flower of war beneath,
Crushing charred limbs and molten arms of men;
So through crushed branches and the reddening brake
Clamoured and crashed the fervour of his feet,
And trampled, springing sideways from the tusk,
Too tardy a moving mould of heavy strength,
Ancaeus; and as flakes of weak-winged snow
Break, all the hard thews of his heaving limbs
Broke, and rent flesh fell every way, and blood
Flew, and fierce fragments of no more a man.
Then all the heroes drew sharp breath, and gazed,
And smote not; but Meleager, but thy son,
Right in the wild way of the coming curse
Rock-rooted, fair with fierce and fastened lips,
Clear eyes, and springing muscle and shortening limb—
With chin aslant indrawn to a tightening throat,
Grave, and with gathered sinews, like a god—
Aimed on the left side his well-handled spear
Grasped where the ash was knottiest hewn, and smote,
And with no missile wound, the monstrous boar
Right in the hairiest hollow of his hide
Under the last rib, sheer through bulk and bone,
Deep in; and deeply smitten, and to death,
The heavy horror with his hanging shafts
Leapt, and fell furiously, and from raging lips
Foamed out the latest wrath of all his life.
And all they praised the gods with mightier heart,
Zeus and all gods, but chiefliest Artemis,
Seeing; but Meleager bade whet knives and flay,

Strip and stretch out the splendour of the spoil;
And hot and horrid from the work all these
Sat, and drew breath and drank and made great cheer
And washed the hard sweat off their calmer brows.
For much sweet grass grew higher than grew the reed,
And good for slumber, and every holier herb,
Narcissus, and the low-lying melilote,
And all of goodliest blade and bloom that springs
Where, hid by heavier hyacinth, violet buds
Blossom and burn; and fire of yellower flowers
And light of crescent lilies, and such leaves
As fear the Faun's and know the Dryad's foot;
Olive and ivy and poplar dedicate,
And many a well-spring overwatched of these.
There now they rest; but me the king bade bear
Good tidings to rejoice this town and thee.
Wherefore be glad, and all ye give much thanks,
For fallen is all the trouble of Calydon.

ALTHAEA

Laud ye the gods; for this they have given is good,
And what shall be they hide until their time.
Much good and somewhat grievous hast thou said,
And either well; but let all sad things be,
Till all have made before the prosperous gods
Burnt-offering, and poured out the floral wine.
Look fair, O gods, and favourable; for we
Praise you with no false heart or flattering mouth,
Being merciful, but with pure souls and prayer.

HERALD

Thou hast prayed well; for whoso fears not these,
But once being prosperous waxes huge of heart,
Him shall some new thing unaware destroy.

245

CHORUS

O that I now, I too were
By deep wells and water-floods,
Streams of ancient hills, and where
All the wan green places bear
Blossoms cleaving to the sod,
Fruitless fruit, and grasses fair,
Or such darkest ivy-buds
As divide thy yellow hair,
Bacchus, and their leaves that nod
Round thy fawnskin brush the bare
Snow-soft shoulders of a god;
There the year is sweet, and there
Earth is full of secret springs,
And the fervent rose-cheeked hours,
Those that marry dawn and noon,
There are sunless, there look pale
In dim leaves and hidden air,
Pale as grass or latter flowers
Or the wild vine's wan wet rings
Full of dew beneath the moon,
And all day the nightingale
Sleeps, and all night sings;
There in cold remote recesses
That nor alien eyes assail,
Feet, nor imminence of wings,
Nor a wind nor any tune,
Thou, O queen and holiest,
Flower the whitest of all things,
With reluctant lengthening tresses
And with sudden splendid breast
Save of maidens unbeholden,

There are wont to enter, there
Thy divine swift limbs and golden
Maiden growth of unbound hair,
Bathed in waters white,
Shine, and many a maid's by thee
In moist woodland or the hilly
Flowerless brakes where wells abound
Out of all men's sight;
Or in lower pools that see
All their marges clothed all round
With the innumerable lily,
Whence the golden-girdled bee
Flits through flowering rush to fret
White or duskier violet,
Fair as those that in far years
With their buds left luminous
And their little leaves made wet,
From the warmer dew of tears,
Mother's tears in extreme need,
Hid the limbs of Iamus,
Of thy brother's seed;
For his heart was piteous
Toward him, even as thine heart now
Pitiful toward us;
Thine, O goddess, turning hither
A benignant blameless brow;
Seeing enough of evil done
And lives withered as leaves wither
In the blasting of the sun;
Seeing enough of hunters dead,
Ruin enough of all our year,
Herds and harvests slain and shed,
Herdsmen stricken many an one,

Fruits and flocks consumed together,
And great length of deadly days.
Yet with reverent lips and fear
Turn we toward thee, turn and praise
For this lightening of clear weather
And prosperities begun.
For not seldom, when all air
As bright water without breath
Shines, and when men fear not, fate
Without thunder unaware
Breaks, and brings down death.
Joy with grief ye great gods give,
Good with bad, and overbear
All the pride of us that live,
All the high estate,
As ye long since overbore,
As in old time long before,
Many a strong man and a great,
All that were.
But do thou, sweet, otherwise,
Having heed of all our prayer,
Taking note of all our sighs;
We beseech thee by thy light,
By thy bow, and thy sweet eyes,
And the kingdom of the night,
Be thou favourable and fair;
By thine arrows and thy might
And Orion overthrown;
By the maiden thy delight,
By the indissoluble zone
And the sacred hair.

MESSENGER

Maidens, if ye will sing now, shift your song,
Bow down, cry, wail for pity; is this a time
For singing? nay, for strewing of dust and ash,
Rent raiment, and for bruising of the breast.

CHORUS

What new thing wolf-like lurks behind thy words?
What snake's tongue in thy lips? what fire in the eyes?

MESSENGER

Bring me before the queen and I will speak.

CHORUS

Lo, she comes forth as from thank-offering made.

MESSENGER

A barren offering for a bitter gift.

ALTHAEA

What are these borne on branches, and the face
Covered? no mean men living, but now slain
Such honour have they, if any dwell with death.

MESSENGER

Queen, thy twain brethren and thy mother's sons.

ALTHAEA

Lay down your dead till I behold their blood
If it be mine indeed, and I will weep.

MESSENGER

Weep if thou wilt, for these men shall no more.

R   249

ALTHAEA

O brethren, O my father's sons, of me
Well loved and well reputed, I should weep
Tears dearer than the dear blood drawn from you
But that I know you not uncomforted,
Sleeping no shameful sleep, however slain,
For my son surely hath avenged you dead.

MESSENGER

Nay, should thine own seed slay himself, O queen?

ALTHAEA

Thy double word brings forth a double death.

MESSENGER

Know this then singly, by one hand they fell.

ALTHAEA

What mutterest thou with thine ambiguous mouth?

MESSENGER

Slain by thy son's hand; is that saying so hard?

ALTHAEA

Our time is come upon us: it is here.

CHORUS

O miserable, and spoiled at thine own hand.

ALTHAEA

Wert thou not called Meleager from this womb?

CHORUS

A grievous huntsman hath it bred to thee.

ATALANTA IN CALYDON

ALTHAEA

Wert thou born fire, and shalt thou not devour?

CHORUS

The fire thou madest, will it consume even thee?

ALTHAEA

My dreams are fallen upon me; burn thou too.

CHORUS

Not without God are visions born and die.

ALTHAEA

The gods are many about me; I am one.

CHORUS

She groans as men wrestling with heavier gods.

ALTHAEA

They rend me, they divide me, they destroy.

CHORUS

Or one labouring in travail of strange births.

ALTHAEA

They are strong, they are strong; I am broken, and these
prevail.

CHORUS

The god is great against her; she will die.

ALTHAEA

Yea, but not now; for my heart too is great.
I would I were not here in sight of the sun.
But thou, speak all thou sawest, and I will die.

MESSENGER

O queen, for queenlike hast thou borne thyself,
A little word may hold so great mischance.
For in division of the sanguine spoil
These men thy brethren wrangling bade yield up
The boar's head and the horror of the hide
That this might stand a wonder in Calydon,
Hallowed; and some drew toward them; but thy son
With great hands grasping all that weight of hair
Cast down the dead heap clanging and collapsed
At female feet, saying This thy spoil not mine,
Maiden, thine own hand for thyself hath reaped,
And all this praise God gives thee: she thereat
Laughed, as when dawn touches the sacred night
The sky sees laugh and redden and divide
Dim lips and eyelids virgin of the sun,
Hers, and the warm slow breasts of morning heave,
Fruitful, and flushed with flame from lamp-lit hours,
And maiden undulation of clear hair
Colour the clouds; so laughed she from pure heart,
Lit with a low blush to the braided hair,
And rose-coloured and cold like very dawn,
Golden and godlike, chastely with chaste lips,
A faint grave laugh; and all they held their peace,
And she passed by them. Then one cried Lo now,
Shall not the Arcadian shoot out lips at us,
Saying all we were despoiled by this one girl?

And all they rode against her violently
And cast the fresh crown from her hair, and now
They had rent her spoil away, dishonouring her,
Save that Meleager, as a tame lion chafed,
Bore on them, broke them, and as fire cleaves wood
So clove and drove them, smitten in twain; but she
Smote not nor heaved up hand; and this man first,
Plexippus, crying out This for love's sake, sweet,
Drove at Meleager, who with spear straightening
Pierced his cheek through; then Toxeus made for him,
Dumb, but his spear spake; vain and violent words.
Fruitless; for him too stricken through both sides
The earth felt falling, and his horse's foam
Blanched thy son's face, his slayer; and these being slain,
None moved nor spake; but Oeneus bade bear hence
These made of heaven infatuate in their deaths,
Foolish; for these would baffle fate, and fell.
And they passed on, and all men honoured her,
Being honourable, as one revered of heaven.

ALTHAEA

What say you, women? is all this not well done?

CHORUS

No man doth well but God hath part in him.

ALTHAEA

But no part here; for these my brethren born
Ye have no part in, these ye know not of
As I that was their sister, a sacrifice
Slain in their slaying. I would I had died for these;
For this man dead walked with me, child by child,

And made a weak staff for my feebler feet
With his own tender wrist and hand, and held
And led me softly and shewed me gold and steel
And shining shapes of mirror and bright crown
And all things fair; and threw light spears, and brought
Young hounds to huddle at my feet and thrust
Tame heads against my little maiden breasts
And please me with great eyes; and those days went
And these are bitter and I a barren queen
And sister miserable, a grievous thing
And mother of many curses; and she too,
My sister Leda, sitting overseas
With fair fruits round her, and her faultless lord,
Shall curse me, saying A sorrow and not a son,
Sister, thou barest, even a burning fire,
A brand consuming thine own soul and me.
But ye now, sons of Thestius, make good cheer,
For ye shall have such wood to funeral fire
As no king hath; and flame that once burnt down
Oil shall not quicken or breath relume or wine
Refresh again; much costlier than fine gold,
And more than many lives of wandering men.

CHORUS

O queen, thou hast yet with thee love-worthy things,
Thine husband, and the great strength of thy son.

ALTHAEA

Who shall get brothers for me while I live?
Who bear them? who bring forth in lieu of these?
Are not our fathers and our brethren one,
And no man like them? are not mine here slain?

Have we not hung together, he and I,
Flowerwise feeding as the feeding bees,
With mother-milk for honey? and this man too,
Dead, with my son's spear thrust between his sides,
Hath he not seen us, later born than he,
Laugh with lips filled, and laughed again for love?
There were no sons then in the world, nor spears,
Nor deadly births of women; but the gods
Allowed us, and our days were clear of these.
I would I had died unwedded, and brought forth
No swords to vex the world; for these that spake
Sweet words long since and loved me will not speak
Nor love nor look upon me; and all my life
I shall not hear nor see them living men.
But I too living, how shall I now live?
What life shall this be with my son, to know
What hath been and desire what will not be,
Look for dead eyes and listen for dead lips,
And kill mine own heart with remembering them,
And with those eyes that see their slayer alive
Weep, and wring hands that clasp him by the hand?
How shall I bear my dreams of them, to hear
False voices, feel the kisses of false mouths
And footless sound of perished feet, and then
Wake and hear only it may be their own hounds
Whine masterless in miserable sleep,
And see their boar-spears and their beds and seats
And all the gear and housings of their lives
And not the men? shall hounds and horses mourn,
Pine with strange eyes, and prick up hungry ears,
Famish and fail at heart for their dear lords,
And I not heed at all? and those blind things
Fall off from life for love's sake, and I live?

255

Surely some death is better than some life,
Better one death for him and these and me.
For if the gods had slain them it may be
I had endured it; if they had fallen by war
Or by the nets and knives of privy death
And by hired hands while sleeping, this thing too
I had set my soul to suffer; or this hunt,
Had this despatched them under tusk or tooth
Torn, sanguine, trodden, broken; for all deaths
Or honourable or with facile feet avenged
And hands of swift gods following, all save this,
Are bearable; but not for their sweet land
Fighting, but not a sacrifice, lo these
Dead; for I had not then shed all mine heart
Out at mine eyes: then either with good speed,
Being just, I had slain their slayer atoningly,
Or strewn with flowers their fire and on their tombs
Hung crowns, and over them a song, and seen
Their praise outflame their ashes: for all men,
All maidens, had come thither, and from pure lips
Shed songs upon them, from heroic eyes
Tears; and their death had been a deathless life;
But now, by no man hired nor alien sword,
By their own kindred are they fallen, in peace,
After much peril, friendless among friends,
By hateful hands they loved; and how shall mine
Touch these returning red and not from war,
These fatal from the vintage of men's veins,
Dead men my brethren? how shall these wash off
No festal stains of undelightful wine,
How mix the blood, my blood on them, with me,
Holding mine hand? or how shall I say, son,
That am no sister? but by night and day

Shall we not sit and hate each other, and think
Things hate-worthy? not live with shamefast eyes,
Brow-beaten, treading soft with fearful feet,
Each unupbraided, each without rebuke
Convicted, and without a word reviled
Each of another? and I shall let thee live
And see thee strong and hear men for thy sake
Praise me, but these thou wouldest not let live
No man shall praise for ever? these shall lie
Dead, unbeloved, unholpen, all through thee?
Sweet were they toward me living, and mine heart
Desired them, but was then well satisfied,
That now is as men hungered; and these dead
I shall want always to the day I die.
For all things else and all men may renew;
Yea, son for son the gods may give and take,
But never a brother or sister any more.

CHORUS

Nay, for the son lies close about thine heart,
Full of thy milk, warm from thy womb, and drains
Life and the blood of life and all thy fruit,
Eats thee and drinks thee as who breaks bread and eats,
Treads wine and drinks, thyself, a sect of thee;
And if he feed not, shall not thy flesh faint?
Or drink not, are not thy lips dead for thirst?
This thing moves more than all things, even thy son,
That thou cleave to him; and he shall honour thee,
Thy womb that bare him and the breasts he knew,
Reverencing most for thy sake all his gods.

ALTHAEA

But these the gods too gave me, and these my son,

Not reverencing his gods nor mine own heart
Nor the old sweet years nor all venerable things,
But cruel, and in his ravin like a beast,
Hath taken away to slay them: yea, and she,
She the strange woman, she the flower, the sword,
Red from spilt blood, a mortal flower to men,
Adorable, detestable—even she
Saw with strange eyes and with strange lips rejoiced,
Seeing these mine own slain of mine own, and me
Made miserable above all miseries made,
A grief among all women in the world,
A name to be washed out with all men's tears.

CHORUS

Strengthen thy spirit; is this not also a god,
Chance, and the wheel of all necessities?
Hard things have fallen upon us from harsh gods,
Whom lest worse hap rebuke we not for these.

ALTHAEA

My spirit is strong against itself, and I
For these things' sake cry out on mine own soul
That it endures outrage, and dolorous days,
And life, and this inexpiable impotence.
Weak am I, weak and shameful; my breath drawn
Shames me, and monstrous things and violent gods.
What shall atone? what heal me? what bring back
Strength to the foot, light to the face? what herb
Assuage me? what restore me? what release?
What strange thing eaten or drunken, O great gods,
Make me as you or as the beasts that feed,
Slay and divide and cherish their own hearts?
For these ye show us; and we less than these

Have not wherewith to live as all these things
Which all their lives fare after their own kind
As who doth well rejoicing; but we ill,
Weeping or laughing, we whom eyesight fails,
Knowledge and light of face and perfect heart,
And hands we lack, and wit; and all our days
Sin, and have hunger, and die infatuated.
For madness have ye given us and not health,
And sins whereof we know not; and for these
Death, and sudden destruction unaware.
What shall we say now? what thing comes of us?

CHORUS

Alas, for all this all men undergo.

ALTHAEA

Wherefore I will not that these twain, O gods,
Die as a dog dies, eaten of creeping things,
Abominable, a loathing; but though dead
Shall they have honour and such funereal flame
As strews men's ashes in their enemies' face
And blinds their eyes who hate them: lest men say,
'Lo, how they lie, and living had great kin,
And none of these hath pity of them, and none
Regards them lying, and none is wrung at heart,
None moved in spirit for them, naked and slain,
Abhorred, abased, and no tears comfort them:'
And in the dark this grieve Eurythemis,
Hearing how these her sons come down to her
Unburied, unavenged, as kinless men,
And had a queen their sister. That were shame
Worse than this grief. Yet how to atone at all
I know not; seeing the love of my born son,

A new-made mother's new-born love, that grows
From the soft child to the strong man, now soft
Now strong as either, and still one sole same love,
Strives with me, no light thing to strive withal;
This love is deep, and natural to man's blood,
And ineffaceable with many tears.
Yet shall not these rebuke me though I die,
Nor she in that waste world with all her dead,
My mother, among the pale flocks fallen as leaves,
Folds of dead people, and alien from the sun;
Nor lack some bitter comfort, some poor praise,
Being queen, to have borne her daughter like a queen,
Righteous; and though mine own fire burn me too,
She shall have honour and these her sons, though dead.
But all the gods will, all they do, and we
Not all we would, yet somewhat; and one choice
We have, to live and do just deeds and die.

CHORUS

Terrible words she communes with, and turns
Swift fiery eyes in doubt against herself,
And murmurs as who talks in dreams with death.

ALTHAEA

For the unjust also dieth, and him all men
Hate, and himself abhors the unrighteousness,
And seeth his own dishonour intolerable.
But I being just, doing right upon myself,
Slay mine own soul, and no man born shames me.
For none constrains nor shall rebuke, being done,
What none compelled me doing; thus these things fare.
Ah, ah, that such things should so fare; ah me,
That I am found to do them and endure,

Chosen and constrained to choose, and bear myself
Mine own wound through mine own flesh to the heart
Violently stricken, a spoiler and a spoil,
A ruin ruinous, fallen on mine own son.
Ah, ah, for me too as for these; alas,
For that is done that shall be, and mine hand
Full of the deed, and full of blood mine eyes,
That shall see never nor touch anything
Save blood unstanched and fire unquenchable.

CHORUS

What wilt thou do? what ails thee? for the house
Shakes ruinously; wilt thou bring fire for it?

ALTHAEA

Fire in the roofs, and on the lintels fire.
Lo ye, who stand and weave, between the doors,
There; and blood drips from hand and thread, and stains
Threshold and raiment and me passing in
Flecked with the sudden sanguine drops of death.

CHORUS

Alas that time is stronger than strong men,
Fate than all gods: and these are fallen on us.

ALTHAEA

A little since and I was glad; and now
I never shall be glad or sad again.

CHORUS

Between two joys a grief grows unaware.

ALTHAEA

A little while and I shall laugh; and then
I shall weep never and laugh not any more.

CHORUS

What shall be said? for words are thorns to grief.
Withhold thyself a little and fear the gods.

ALTHAEA

Fear died when these were slain; and I am as dead,
And fear is of the living; these fear none.

CHORUS

Have pity upon all people for their sake.

ALTHAEA

It is done now; shall I put back my day?

CHORUS

An end is come, an end; this is of God.

ALTHAEA

I am fire, and burn myself; keep clear of fire.

CHORUS

The house is broken, is broken; it shall not stand.

ALTHAEA

Woe, woe for him that breaketh; and a rod
Smote it of old, and now the axe is here.

CHORUS

Not as with sundering of the earth
  Nor as with cleaving of the sea
Nor fierce foreshadowings of a birth
  Nor flying dreams of death to be
Nor loosening of the large world's girth
And quickening of the body of night,
  And sound of thunder in men's ears
And fire of lightning in men's sight,
  Fate, mother of desires and fears,
  Bore unto men the law of tears;
But sudden, an unfathered flame,
  And broken out of night, she shone,
She, without body, without name,
  In days forgotten and foregone;
And heaven rang round her as she came
Like smitten cymbals, and lay bare;
  Clouds and great stars, thunders and snows,
The blue sad fields and folds of air,
  The life that breathes, the life that grows,
  All wind, all fire, that burns or blows,
Even all these knew her: for she is great;
  The daughter of doom, the mother of death,
The sister of sorrow; a lifelong weight
  That no man's finger lighteneth,
Nor any god can lighten fate;
A landmark seen across the way
  Where one race treads as the other trod;
An evil sceptre, an evil stay,
  Wrought for a staff, wrought for a rod,
  The bitter jealousy of God.

For death is deep as the sea,
    And fate as the waves thereof.
Shall the waves take pity on thee
    Or the south wind offer thee love?
Wilt thou take the night for thy day
Or the darkness for light on thy way,
    Till thou say in thine heart Enough?
Behold, thou art over fair, thou art over wise;
The sweetness of spring in thine hair, and the light in
                                            thine eyes.
The light of the spring in thine eyes, and the sound in
                                            thine ears;
Yet thine heart shall wax heavy with sighs and thine
                                            eyelids with tears.
Wilt thou cover thine hair with gold, and with silver
                                            thy feet?
Hast thou taken the purple to fold thee, and made thy
                                            mouth sweet?
Behold, when thy face is made bare, he that loved thee
                                            shall hate;
Thy face shall be no more fair at the fall of thy fate.
For thy life shall fall as a leaf and be shed as the rain;
And the veil of thine head shall be grief; and the crown
                                            shall be pain.

ALTHAEA

Ho, ye that wail, and ye that sing, make way
Till I be come among you. Hide your tears,
Ye little weepers, and you laughing lips,
Ye laughers for a little; lo, mine eyes
That outweep heaven at rainiest, and my mouth
That laughs as gods laugh at us. Fate's are we,
Yet fate is ours a breathing-space; yea, mine,

Fate is made mine for ever; he is my son,
My bedfellow, my brother. You strong gods,
Give place unto me; I am as any of you,
To give life and to take life. Thou, old earth,
That hast made man and unmade; thou whose mouth
Looks red from the eaten fruits of thine own womb;
Behold me with what lips upon what food
I feed and fill my body; even with flesh
Made of my body. Lo, the fire I lit
I burn with fire to quench it; yea, with flame
I burn up even the dust and ash thereof.

CHORUS

Woman, what fire is this thou burnest with?

ALTHAEA

Yea to the bone, yea to the blood and all.

CHORUS

For this thy face and hair are as one fire.

ALTHAEA

A tongue that licks and beats upon the dust.

CHORUS

And in thine eyes are hollow light and heat.

ALTHAEA

Of flame not fed with hand or frankincense.

CHORUS

I fear thee for the trembling of thine eyes.

ALTHAEA

Neither with love they tremble nor for fear.

CHORUS

And thy mouth shuddering like a shot bird.

ALTHAEA

Not as the bride's mouth when man kisses it.

CHORUS

Nay, but what thing is this thing thou hast done?

ALTHAEA

Look, I am silent, speak your eyes for me.

CHORUS

I see a faint fire lightening from the hall.

ALTHAEA

Gaze, stretch your eyes, strain till the lids drop off.

CHORUS

Flushed pillars down the flickering vestibule.

ALTHAEA

Stretch with your necks like birds: cry, chirp as they.

CHORUS

And a long brand that blackens: and white dust.

ALTHAEA

O children, what is this ye see? your eyes
Are blinder than night's face at fall of moon.
That is my son, my flesh, my fruit of life,

My travail, and the year's weight of my womb,
Meleager, a fire enkindled of mine hands
And of mine hands extinguished; this is he.

CHORUS

O gods, what word has flown out at thy mouth?

ALTHAEA

I did this and I say this and I die.

CHORUS

Death stands upon the doorway of thy lips,
And in thy mouth has death set up his house.

ALTHAEA

O death, a little, a little while, sweet death,
Until I see the brand burnt down and die.

CHORUS

She reels as any reed under the wind,
And cleaves unto the ground with staggering feet.

ALTHAEA

Girls, one thing will I say and hold my peace.
I that did this will weep not nor cry out,
Cry ye and weep: I will not call on gods,
Call ye on them; I will not pity man,
Shew ye your pity. I know not if I live;
Save that I feel the fire upon my face
And on my cheek the burning of a brand.
Yea the smoke bites me, yea I drink the steam
With nostril and with eyelid and with lip
Insatiate and intolerant; and mine hands

Burn, and fire feeds upon mine eyes; I reel
As one made drunk with living, whence he draws
Drunken delight; yet I, though mad for joy,
Loathe my long living and am waxen red
As with the shadow of shed blood; behold,
I am kindled with the flames that fade in him,
I am swollen with subsiding of his veins,
I am flooded with his ebbing; my lit eyes
Flame with the falling fire that leaves his lids
Bloodless; my cheek is luminous with blood
Because his face is ashen. Yet, O child,
Son, first-born, fairest—O sweet mouth, sweet eyes,
That drew my life out through my suckling breast,
That shone and clove mine heart through—O soft knees
Clinging, O tender treadings of soft feet,
Cheeks warm with little kissings—O child, child,
What have we made each other? Lo, I felt
Thy weight cleave to me, a burden of beauty, O son,
Thy cradled brows and loveliest loving lips,
The floral hair, the little lightening eyes,
And all thy goodly glory; with mine hands
Delicately I fed thee, with my tongue
Tenderly spake, saying, Verily in God's time,
For all the little likeness of thy limbs,
Son, I shall make thee a kingly man to fight,
A lordly leader; and hear before I die,
'She bore the goodliest sword of all the world.'
Oh! Oh! For all my life turns round on me;
I am severed from myself, my name is gone,
My name that was a healing, it is changed,
My name is a consuming. From this time,
Though mine eyes reach to the end of all these things,
My lips shall not unfasten till I die.

SEMI-CHORUS

She has filled with sighing the city,
   And the ways thereof with tears;
She arose, she girdled her sides,
She set her face as a bride's;
She wept, and she had no pity;
   Trembled, and felt no fears.

SEMI-CHORUS

Her eyes were clear as the sun,
   Her brows were fresh as the day;
She girdled herself with gold,
Her robes were manifold;
But the days of her worship are done,
   Her praise is taken away.

SEMI-CHORUS

For she set her hand to the fire,
   With her mouth she kindled the same;
As the mouth of a flute-player,
So was the mouth of her;
With the might of her strong desire
   She blew the breath of the flame.

SEMI-CHORUS

She set her hand to the wood,
   She took the fire in her hand;
As one who is nigh to death,
She panted with strange breath;
She opened her lips unto blood,
   She breathed and kindled the brand.

SEMI-CHORUS

As a wood-dove newly shot,
　　She sobbed and lifted her breast;
She sighed and covered her eyes,
Filling her lips with sighs;
She sighed, she withdrew herself not,
　　She refrained not, taking not rest.

SEMI-CHORUS

But as the wind which is drouth,
　　And as the air which is death,
As storm that severeth ships,
Her breath severing her lips,
The breath came forth of her mouth
　　And the fire came forth of her breath.

SECOND MESSENGER

Queen, and you maidens, there is come on us
A thing more deadly than the face of death;
Meleager the good lord is as one slain.

SEMI-CHORUS

Without sword, without sword is he stricken;
　　Slain, and slain without hand.

SECOND MESSENGER

For as keen ice divided of the sun
His limbs divide, and as thawed snow the flesh
Thaws from off all his body to the hair.

SEMI-CHORUS

He wastes as the embers quicken;
　　With the brand he fades as a brand.

SECOND MESSENGER

Even while they sang and all drew hither and he
Lifted both hands to crown the Arcadian's hair
And fix the looser leaves, both hands fell down.

SEMI-CHORUS

With rending of cheek and of hair
Lament ye, mourn for him, weep.

SECOND MESSENGER

Straightway the crown slid off and smote on earth,
First fallen; and he, grasping his own hair, groaned
And cast his raiment round his face and fell.

SEMI-CHORUS

Alas for visions that were,
And soothsayings spoken in sleep.

SECOND MESSENGER

But the king twitched his reins in and leapt down
And caught him, crying out twice 'O child' and
                                    thrice,
So that men's eyelids thickened with their tears.

SEMI-CHORUS

Lament with a long lamentation,
Cry, for an end is at hand.

SECOND MESSENGER

O son, he said, son, lift thine eyes, draw breath,
Pity me; but Meleager with sharp lips
Gasped, and his face waxed like as sunburnt grass.

SEMI/CHORUS

Cry aloud, O thou kingdom, O nation,
O stricken, a ruinous land.

SECOND MESSENGER

Whereat king Oeneus, straightening feeble knees,
With feeble hands heaved up a lessening weight,
And laid him sadly in strange hands, and wept.

SEMI/CHORUS

Thou art smitten, her lord, her desire,
Thy dear blood wasted as rain.

SECOND MESSENGER

And they with tears and rendings of the beard
Bear hither a breathing body, wept upon
And lightening at each footfall, sick to death.

SEMI/CHORUS

Thou madest thy sword as a fire,
With fire for a sword thou art slain.

SECOND MESSENGER

And lo, the feast turned funeral, and the crowns
Fallen; and the huntress and the hunter trapped;
And weeping and changed faces and veiled hair.

MELEAGER

Let your hands meet
Round the weight of my head;
Lift ye my feet
As the feet of the dead;
For the flesh of my body is molten, the limbs of it molten
as lead.

CHORUS

O thy luminous face,
　　Thine imperious eyes!
O the grief, O the grace,
　　As of day when it dies!
Who is this bending over thee, lord, with tears and
　　　　suppression of sighs?

MELEAGER

Is a bride so fair?
　　Is a maid so meek?
With unchapleted hair,
　　With unfilleted cheek,
Atalanta, the pure among women, whose name is as
　　　　blessing to speak.

ATALANTA

I would that with feet
　　Unsandalled, unshod,
Overbold, overfleet,
　　I had swum not nor trod
From Arcadia to Calydon northward, a blast of the
　　　　envy of God.

MELEAGER

Unto each man his fate;
　　Unto each as he saith
In whose fingers the weight
　　Of the world is as breath;
Yet I would that in clamour of battle mine hands had
　　　　laid hold upon death.

CHORUS
Not with cleaving of shields
And their clash in thine ear,
When the lord of fought fields
Breaketh spearshaft from spear,
Thou art broken, our lord, thou art broken, with travail
and labour and fear.

MELEAGER
Would God he had found me
Beneath fresh boughs!
Would God he had bound me
Unawares in mine house,
With light in mine eyes, and songs in my lips, and a
crown on my brows!

CHORUS
Whence art thou sent from us?
Whither thy goal?
How art thou rent from us,
Thou that wert whole,
As with severing of eyelids and eyes, as with sundering
of body and soul!

MELEAGER
My heart is within me
As an ash in the fire;
Whosoever hath seen me,
Without lute, without lyre,
Shall sing of me grievous things, even things that were
ill to desire.

CHORUS

Who shall raise thee
From the house of the dead?
Or what man praise thee
That thy praise may be said?
Alas thy beauty! alas thy body! alas thine head!

MELEAGER

But thou, O mother,
The dreamer of dreams,
Wilt thou bring forth another
To feel the sun's beams
When I move among shadows a shadow, and wail by
impassable streams?

OENEUS

What thing wilt thou leave me
Now this thing is done?
A man wilt thou give me,
A son for my son,
For the light of mine eyes, the desire of my life, the desir-
able one?

CHORUS

Thou wert glad above others,
Yea, fair beyond word;
Thou wert glad among mothers;
For each man that heard
Of thee, praise there was added unto thee, as wings to
the feet of a bird.

OENEUS

Who shall give back
Thy face of old years
With travail made black,
Grown grey among fears,
Mother of sorrow, mother of cursing, mother of tears?

MELEAGER

Though thou art as fire
Fed with fuel in vain,
My delight, my desire,
Is more chaste than the rain,
More pure than the dewfall, more holy than stars are that
live without stain.

ATALANTA

I would that as water
My life's blood had thawn,
Or as winter's wan daughter
Leaves lowland and lawn
Spring-stricken, or ever mine eyes had beheld thee made
dark in thy dawn.

CHORUS

When thou dravest the men
Of the chosen of Thrace,
None turned him again
Nor endured he thy face
Clothed round with the blush of the battle, with light
from a terrible place.

OENEUS

Thou shouldst die as he dies
For whom none sheddeth tears;
Filling thine eyes
And fulfilling thine ears
With the brilliance of battle, the bloom and the beauty,
the splendour of spears.

CHORUS

In the ears of the world
It is sung, it is told,
And the light thereof hurled
And the noise thereof rolled
From the Acroceraunian snow to the ford of the fleece
of gold.

MELEAGER

Would God ye could carry me
Forth of all these;
Heap sand and bury me
By the Chersonese
Where the thundering Bosphorus answers the thunder of
Pontic seas.

OENEUS

Dost thou mock at our praise
And the singing begun
And the men of strange days
Praising my son
In the folds of the hills of home, high places of Calydon?

MELEAGER

For the dead man no home is;
　　Ah, better to be
What the flower of the foam is
　　In fields of the sea,
That the sea-waves might be as my raiment, the gulf-
　　　　stream a garment for me.

CHORUS

Who shall seek thee and bring
　　And restore thee thy day,
When the dove dipt her wing
　　And the oars won their way
Where the narrowing Symplegades whitened the straits
　　　　of Propontis with spray?

MELEAGER

Will ye crown me my tomb
　　Or exalt me my name,
Now my spirits consume,
　　Now my flesh is a flame?
Let the sea slake it once, and men speak of me sleeping to
　　　　praise me or shame.

CHORUS

Turn back now, turn thee,
　　As who turns him to wake;
Though the life in thee burn thee,
　　Couldst thou bathe it and slake
Where the sea-ridge of Helle hangs heavier, and east
　　　　upon west waters break?

MELEAGER

Would the winds blow me back
Or the waves hurl me home?
Ah, to touch in the track
Where the pine learnt to roam
Cold girdles and crowns of the sea-gods, cool blossoms
of water and foam!

CHORUS

The gods may release
That they made fast;
Thy soul shall have ease
In thy limbs at the last;
But what shall they give thee for life, sweet life that is
overpast?

MELEAGER

Not the life of men's veins,
Not of flesh that conceives;
But the grace that remains,
The fair beauty that cleaves
To the life of the rains in the grasses, the life of the dews
on the leaves.

CHORUS

Thou wert helmsman and chief;
Wilt thou turn in an hour,
Thy limbs to the leaf,
Thy face to the flower,
Thy blood to the water, thy soul to the gods who divide
and devour?

MELEAGER

The years are hungry,
    They wail all their days;
The gods wax angry
    And weary of praise;
And who shall bridle their lips? and who shall straiten
                            their ways?

CHORUS

The gods guard over us
    With sword and with rod;
Weaving shadow to cover us,
    Heaping the sod,
That law may fulfil herself wholly, to darken man's face
                        before God.

MELEAGER

O holy head of Oeneus, lo thy son
Guiltless, yet red from alien guilt, yet foul
With kinship of contaminated lives,
Lo, for their blood I die; and mine own blood
For bloodshedding of mine is mixed therewith,
That death may not discern me from my kin.
Yet with clean heart I die and faultless hand,
Not shamefully; thou therefore of thy love
Salute me, and bid fare among the dead
Well, as the dead fare; for the best man dead
Fares sadly; nathless I now faring well
Pass without fear where nothing is to fear
Having thy love about me and thy goodwill,
O father, among dark places and men dead.

OENEUS

Child, I salute thee with sad heart and tears,
And bid thee comfort, being a perfect man
In fight, and honourable in the house of peace.
The gods give thee fair wage and dues of death,
And me brief days and ways to come at thee.

MELEAGER

Pray thou thy days be long before thy death,
And full of ease and kingdom; seeing in death
There is no comfort and none aftergrowth,
Nor shall one thence look up and see day's dawn
Nor light upon the land whither I go.
Live thou and take thy fill of days and die
When thy day comes; and make not much of death
Lest ere thy day thou reap an evil thing.
Thou too, the bitter mother and mother-plague
Of this my weary body—thou too, queen,
The source and end, the sower and the scythe,
The rain that ripens and the drought that slays,
The sand that swallows and the spring that feeds,
To make me and unmake me—thou, I say,
Althaea, since my father's ploughshare, drawn
Through fatal seedland of a female field,
Furrowed thy body, whence a wheaten ear
Strong from the sun and fragrant from the rains
I sprang and cleft the closure of thy womb,
Mother, I dying with unforgetful tongue
Hail thee as holy and worship thee as just
Who art unjust and unholy; and with my knees
Would worship, but thy fire and subtlety,
Dissundering them, devour me; for these limbs

Are as light dust and crumblings from mine urn
Before the fire has touched them; and my face
As a dead leaf or dead foot's mark on snow,
And all this body a broken barren tree
That was so strong, and all this flower of life
Disbranched and desecrated miserably,
And minished all that god-like muscle and might
And lesser than a man's: for all my veins
Fail me, and all mine ashen life burns down.
I would thou hadst let me live; but gods averse,
But fortune, and the fiery feet of change,
And time, these would not, these tread out my life,
These and not thou; me too thou hast loved, and I
Thee; but this death was mixed with all my life,
Mine end with my beginning: and this law,
This only, slays me, and not my mother at all.
And let no brother or sister grieve too sore,
Nor melt their hearts out on me with their tears,
Since extreme love and sorrowing overmuch
Vex the great gods, and overloving men
Slay and are slain for love's sake; and this house
Shall bear much better children; why should these
Weep? but in patience let them live their lives
And mine pass by forgotten: thou alone,
Mother, thou sole and only, thou not these,
Keep me in mind a little when I die
Because I was thy first-born; let thy soul
Pity me, pity even me gone hence and dead,
Though thou wert wroth, and though thou bear again
Much happier sons, and all men later born
Exceedingly excel me; yet do thou
Forget not, nor think shame; I was thy son.
Time was I did not shame thee; and time was

I thought to live and make thee honourable
With deeds as great as these men's; but they live,
These, and I die; and what thing should have been
Surely I know not; yet I charge thee, seeing
I am dead already, love me not the less,
Me, O my mother; I charge thee by these gods,
My father's, and that holier breast of thine,
By these that see me dying, and that which nursed,
Love me not less, thy first-born: though grief come,
Grief only, of me, and of all these great joy,
And shall come always to thee; for thou knowest,
O mother, O breasts that bare me, for ye know,
O sweet head of my mother, sacred eyes,
Ye know my soul albeit I sinned, ye know
Albeit I kneel not neither touch thy knees,
But with my lips I kneel, and with my heart
I fall about thy feet and worship thee.
And ye farewell now, all my friends; and ye,
Kinsmen, much younger and glorious more than I,
Sons of my mother's sister; and all farewell
That were in Colchis with me, and bare down
The waves and wars that met us: and though times
Change, and though now I be not anything,
Forget not me among you, what I did
In my good time; for even by all those days,
Those days and this, and your own living souls,
And by the light and luck of you that live,
And by this miserable spoil, and me
Dying, I beseech you, let my name not die.
But thou, dear, touch me with thy rose-like hands,
And fasten up mine eyelids with thy mouth,
A bitter kiss; and grasp me with thine arms,
Printing with heavy lips my light waste flesh,

Made light and thin by heavy-handed fate,
And with thine holy maiden eyes drop dew,
Drop tears of dew upon me who am dead,
Me who have loved thee; seeing without sin done
I am gone down to the empty weary house
Where no flesh is nor beauty nor swift eyes
Nor sound of mouth nor might of hands and feet.
But thou, dear, hide my body with thy veil,
And with thy raiment cover foot and head,
And stretch thyself upon me and touch hands
With hands and lips with lips: be pitiful
As thou art maiden perfect; let no man
Defile me to despise me, saying, This man
Died woman-wise, a woman's offering, slain
Through female fingers in his woof of life,
Dishonourable; for thou hast honoured me.
And now for God's sake kiss me once and twice
And let me go; for the night gathers me,
And in the night shall no man gather fruit.

ATALANTA

Hail thou: but I with heavy face and feet
Turn homeward and am gone out of thine eyes.

CHORUS

Who shall contend with his lords
    Or cross them or do them wrong?
Who shall bind them as with cords?
    Who shall tame them as with song?
Who shall smite them as with swords?
    For the hands of their kingdom are strong.

INDEX OF FIRST LINES